THE NORTH WALES PATH
and Ten Selected Walks

The North Wales Path

and Ten Selected Walks

Dave Salter
Dave Worrall

ISBN: 0-86381-546-4

Cover design: Alan Jones

First published in 1999 by
Gwasg Carreg Gwalch, 12 Iard yr Orsaf, Llanrwst, Wales LL26 0EH
℡ 01492 642031   📠 01492 641502
📧 books@carreg-gwalch.co.uk   Internet: www.carreg-gwalch.co.uk

To Caroline, Jo and Susie:
this time their footsteps went with us.

And for those others who have walked
the same way.
You know who you are.

A final thanks to Mike who only got to read it.

CONTENTS

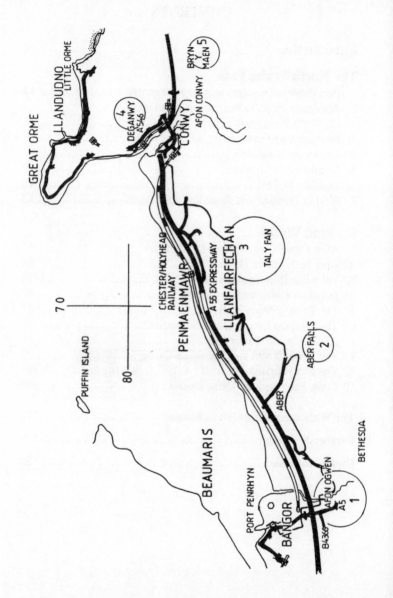

GREAT ORME

LLANDUDNO
LITTLE ORME

BEAUMARIS

PUFFIN ISLAND

80

70

DEGANWY
A546
4

CONWY

BRYN
Y
MAEN 5

AFON CONWY

CHESTER/HOLYHEAD
RAILWAY

A55 EXPRESSWAY

PENMAENMAWR

LLANFAIRFECHAN

TAL Y FAN
3

ABER FALLS
2

ABER

PORT PENRHYN

BANGOR

AFON OGWEN
A5
1

B4366

BETHESDA

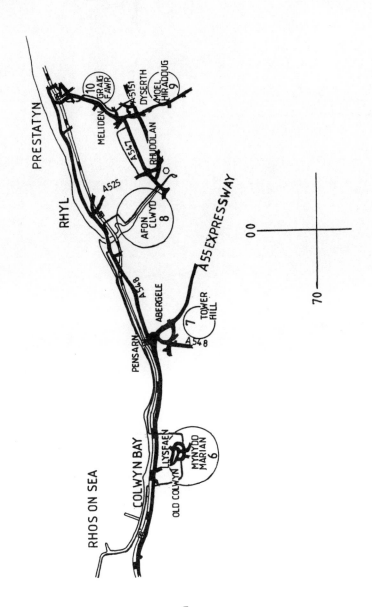

INTRODUCTION

We have always enjoyed the idea of walking long distance footpaths. Sadly for most of us the opportunity to take several days off in one stretch to complete such a path may not present itself. Therefore, when we first came across the North Wales Path it seemed to be an opportunity to walk a long distance path that existed on our own doorstep. It was also apparent that it could be tackled in several ways and this book reflects the different ways the walk can be accomplished. First of all it could be walked in a single push, a walk of sixty miles, that could be achieved in as little as four days or for those who wish to explore along the way in a more leisurely seven days. For those who have the time it would make an acceptable weeks holiday. Also it could be tackled in day excursions, eventually tying all the sections together to create a whole, and lastly it could act as a basis for exploring parts of this coast. The guide therefore attempts to be all things to all men, letting you choose how you wish to walk it. The first part of the book covers the walk in its entirety from Bangor to Prestatyn breaking the walk up into day sections. At the end of each section information is given on how to return to your start point or where to stay in order to carry on the next day. Sadly, the number of campsites may make it difficult to backpack, whereas there are always B and B's to be found. The second section is of individual walks based around the area which can be enjoyed in their own right, and explore areas away from the North Wales Path. These walks introduce some of the less well frequented parts of the coast. Those who take these paths may be surprised by some notable omissions, including Mynydd Conwy, the Great Orme and the Little Orme. These have been covered so well by previous publications that we have left them in favour of some little known walks which we felt deserved inclusion. Our delight in this area came from the surprises rather than the known treasures. Finally, in the third section the route is given from Prestatyn to Bangor for those who may find it easier to complete it this way around.

The path itself is the initiative of the authorities of Gwynedd, Conwy and Denbighshire with input from the Snowdonia National

Park and the Countryside Council for Wales. In its traverse of the North Wales coast, the path passes through varied and diverse countryside which reflects the nature of this coast, from the high mountains to the flat plains, from small villages to towns. If the intention was to show every aspect that North Wales has to offer, then it succeeds. The walk begins in the city of Bangor and soon moves on to the northern flanks of the Carneddau. It traverses these to the moorlands above Llanfairfechan and Penmaenmawr before moving into the limestone country of the Great and Little Ormes. Promenades feature strongly in the middle section, with the occasional foray back into the hills such as above Llysfaen, then on to the coastal flood plain. Before its termination in Prestatyn, the ridge taken by Offa's Dyke is reached and its flanks are used to sneak you into Prestatyn without making you feel that you are entering into the town.

The start and finish points for the walk do not have any historical reasons to connect them, and although the Romans probably passed this way, there is no ancient route to follow. None the less the walk has many interesting aspects and can provide pleasant excursions along a coast that might not initially be considered as an obvious choice for a days walking. That it is full of history and interest is without doubt, but good walking? There is only one way to find out! So pull on the boots and do a little exploring, after all, it may be too wet to walk in Snowdonia today.

Please note:

R	denotes 90° right hand turn
L	denotes 90° left hand turn
½R	denotes 45°right hand turn
½L	denotes 45° left hand turn

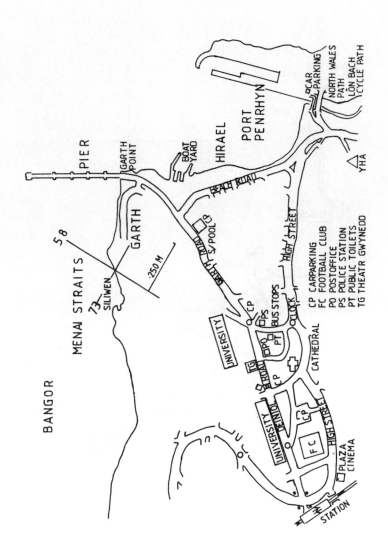

BANGOR

MENAI STRAITS

PIER

GARTH

GARTH POINT

BOAT YARD

HIRAEL

PORT PENRHYN

CAR PARKING

NORTH WALES PATH
LÔN BACH CYCLE PATH

YHA

BEACH ROAD

SILIWEN

250 M

GARTH ROAD

S'POOL CP

CP

PS

BUS STOPS

HIGH STREET

CLOCK

UNIVERSITY

PO

PT

TG

CP

CATHEDRAL

CP CARPARKING
FC FOOTBALL CLUB
PO POSTOFFICE
PS POLICE STATION
PT PUBLIC TOILETS
TG THEATR GWYNEDD

UNIVERSITY DEINIOL

CP

FC

HIGH STREET

PLAZA CINEMA

STATION

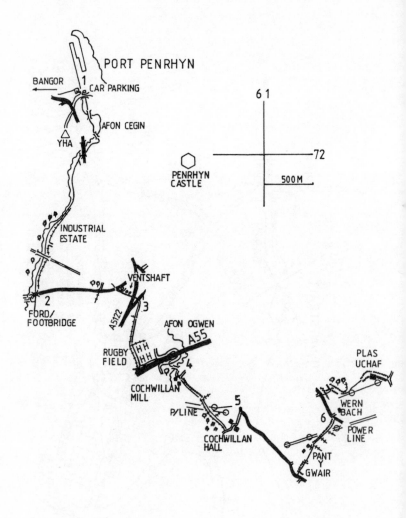

PORT PENRHYN

BANGOR ← 1 CAR PARKING

AFON CEGIN

YHA

INDUSTRIAL ESTATE

VENTSHAFT

2
FORD/ FOOTBRIDGE

A5122

3

AFON OGWEN

A55

RUGBY FIELD

4

COCHWILLAN MILL

P/LINE

COCHWILLAN HALL

5

PANT Y GWAIR

6

PLAS UCHAF

WERN BACH

POWER LINE

61

72

500M

PENRHYN CASTLE

12

Porth Penrhyn (Bangor) to Abergwyngregyn

Maps	1:50.000 Landranger sheet 115 Bangor and Caernarfon; or 1:25.000 Outdoor Leisure sheet 17 Snowdon and Conwy
Distance	11 miles/17.5 kilometres
Height gained	940ft/286metres
Duration	6 hours
Terrain	Good and hard, no real wet patches, walking on the flanks of the Carneddau.
Car Park	For the walk start, park in Porth Penrhyn close to a small building just after crossing the bridge onto the Quays at G.R. 593727.

For the walk finish, park at Bont Newydd out of Abergwyngregyn village towards the falls at G.R. 662720.

The walk starts at Porth Penrhyn in the old area of Hirael (Bangor's Tiger Bay). For those starting from the railway or bus stations, the attraction of passing through the centre of Bangor should add interest to the beginning.

Points of Interest:

Bangor has a long and varied history, and although it has seen many skirmishes in its time, it has never been a fortified city. Instead, Bangor's history is firmly tied to that of the developing church and religion. First of all, it is important to establish that Bangor has a cathedral, and hence is entitled to be called a city. The old city was centred around the early monastic settlement which was later to become the Cathedral of Saint Deiniol. In the 6th century, Deiniol received a gift of land from Maelgwn Gwynedd, which enabled him to build a sanctuary in Bangor and thus establish the first religious settlement. This first Cathedral, which Maelgwn helped to construct, was destroyed in 1071 during the reign of William I. Later it was rebuilt only to be destroyed again by the army of King John in 1212. The Cathedral was once more rebuilt and also enlarged, this time the work was undertaken by Bishop Ainan. In 1277, the Black Friars settled in the area on land granted to them by Bishop Ainan, but unfortunately the house in which they resided was destroyed by fire. The Cathedral itself was again raised to the ground, this time by Owain Glyndwr in 1402. The Cathedral lay in ruins until 1500, when Bishop Henry Deane and Dean Richard Kyffin effected its reconstruction According to legend, during this period of reconstruction, the Cathedral bells were stolen, but when the thief went to the nearby shore to watch his loot being loaded onto a ship for transportation, he was struck down by blindness and the bells, needless to say were soon returned. The history of Bangor and its Cathedral seems to be one of building followed by ruin and damage, gladly this cycle seems to have been broken and the Cathedral is entering a period of restoration where it is being returned to its former glory.

As you walk further towards Porth Penrhyn, you enter the communities which were the maritime areas of the city. These were known as Garth, situated around the area where the Victorian pier now stands and the Hirael community situated around the estuary of Afon Cegin. Shipbuilding was the foundation of these communities, from the late 1700's when small skiffs were built here and later when schooners of up to one hundred and twenty tons were constructed. These larger vessels were built to sail the oceans of the world with their cargo of slate. All the equipment needed to supply these vessels was produced locally, with sail makers, block makers, ship wrights and foundries all existing nearby. Unfortunately, little evidence of this trade now remains except in the minds of the few who remember the ships which used leave the port of Penrhyn with their cargo of slate, and in the paintings of Scott Metcalfe of Penrhyn quay.

During the Victorian era great efforts were made to establish Bangor as a tourist area. At one time, visitors were encouraged to take a dip in the nearby Menai Straits, but this was described by the local gentry as a 'gross outrage to public decency' and therefore families were inhibited from partaking of this simple pleasure. On 12th June 1858, a meeting of local business men was held and a recommendation was made to provide an area suitable for sea bathing. This was to be at Siliwen (close to the present day pier) which had a sheltered gravel beach. In June 1878 a private company started a passenger service running ferries between Bangor, Porthaethwy (Menai Bridge) and Beaumaris, using the twin screw steamer named 'Menai'. During the summer of 1888 the steam ship Alexandra was operating daily sailings from Liverpool calling at Llandudno, Beaumaris, Bangor and Menai Bridge. In August 1889 it was suggested at a meeting that the tourist trade was handicapped by the lack of a pier; passengers of the steamer services having to transfer to small boats in order to be brought ashore. September 1894 saw the appointment of J J Webster, the civil engineer given the task of constructing a pier, close to the site of the ferry area known as Bishops Crossing. The pier was officially opened by Lord Penrhyn on the 14th May 1896. The pier is some 1550 feet long (470 metres) and 25 feet wide (7 metres), with kiosks built along its length. The weekend following the official opening some two and a half thousand promenaders visited the pier at a charge of 2 old pence each, and were entertained by brass bands and numerous street artists.

Another famous event in the history of the area of the Garth pier took place in 1867. Hundreds of Bangor residents flocked to the hillside at Garth to witness John Rees of Machynlleth walking on water. This he announced he would do 'without losing equilibrium'. When Rees arrived wearing a pneumatic oilskin suit, the applause of the crowd was deafening. He sat in the shallows, took two small oars from the pocket of the suit and, in a sitting position commenced to row himself over to the Ynys Môn shore. It was said that the cheers from the assembled crowd rattled windows up to half a mile (800 metres) away. On his return to Garth he lounged nonchalantly in the shallows, explaining his invention. The emphasis was on the safety for mariners that such a device could bring, and this design for a pneumatic belt could claim to be first lifejacket. Unfortunately no more was heard of Mr Rees or his inventions.

After crossing Afon Ogwen, the walk enters the Cochwillan Estate, now part of the Penrhyn Estate. The estate comprises of a mill, a family farm and Cochwillan hall. This is one the finest and largest hall type houses in the area. It was constructed in the late 15th century for the family of Gwilym ap Gruffudd. Gwilym was made Sheriff of Caernarfon by Henry VII, in recognition of Gwilym's part in Henry

VII victory at the battle of Bosworth. After Gwilym ap Gruffudd's death the estate fell into decline, until it was bought in 1622 by John Williams, Archbishop of York and cousin to the Cochwillan family. Following his death in 1650 the hall became a farm house and when the present farm was built, the hall itself became a hay barn. It remained in this condition until 1969 when it was restored to its former glory.

Undoubtedly, it would be difficult to ignore the dominant presence of Penrhyn Castle. For much of this walk it is a major part of the landscape stretched out beneath you. This pseudo Norman castle has a fascinating history which we would strongly recommend you investigate for yourself.

Visually one of the attractions of this walk must be the sight of the spectacular Rhaeadr Fawr and Rhaeadr Fach water falls. Rhaeadr Fawr is also known as the Aber falls, where Afon Goch descends in an impressive fall of 120 feet (37 metres). Here, the river changes name to Afon Rhaeadr Fawr and passes through an area which was once one of the great forests of North Wales. This area is known as Coedydd Aber, and is a National Nature Reserve. A small seasonal exhibition at Nant Cottage, on the route of the walk, shows the natural history of the area and is worth a visit.

Walk 1. R out of the car park and under the road bridge. After passing under the second road bridge (carrying the main road) go L and take the lower of two paths. **2.** After passing under the fourth bridge from the start, turn R onto minor road and R over a bridge. Up minor road to kissing gate on R (small wood on R just after gate). R through kissing gate, and uphill keeping fence and wood on L for 70 metres to where wood bends away to the L. Now continue with hedge on L (passing vent for railway), to join main road. **3.** Cross main road and down path. Cross minor road and R along lane. At end of lane, through kissing gate and continue, keeping hedge on R. Over metal stile and continue along Rugby Club boundary with hedge still on R. At end of rugby field (path junction) go L and parallel with Expressway to kissing gate. Through gate and down service road passing under Expressway. Ascend lane to break in crash barrier. **4.** L down path to footbridge. Over bridge, and continue to edge of the building Felin Cochwillan (mill). L along lane for 35 metres. R through entrance gate and ½ L uphill, keeping wall on L. Through kissing gate and continue with wall on L passing over small track. When path enters field, continue on, with slate fence and wood on R. Through three kissing gates. **5.** At lane, through kissing gate and L, passing through Cochwillan farm, and along track to minor road. R up minor road passing lane to Pant-y-gwair; continue on for a further 120 metres to a kissing gate on L. Through kissing gate, and cross field to next kissing gate. Through this and continue on with wall/fence on L. At field corner, through gap in old wall, and R down into undergrowth, L over metal stile and up to telegraph pole. Continue on until path dips to field gate (close to large house). Do not go through gate but continue with wall on L, passing through kissing gate and continue on with wall/fence on L until a minor road is reached. **6.** L down minor road for 120 metres passing lane to Wern Bach. R over wall stile and through small woods, over stream and up field, keeping wall on L, to top corner. L through kissing gate and then R up lane to Plas Uchaf. Through farm and continue to minor road. At minor road, go L and along to stile and gate on R marked Caerffynnon Cottage. Over stile and ½ L along track. Keep on along track which passes through gates and contours around hillside until later the track passes through a wood plantation. **7.** The track bears R and continues to contour around to give views of the water falls (Rhaeadr Fawr and Rhaeadr Fach). Continue along the now descending path, passing through an area of hawthorn bushes. At field gate the track terminates and continues as a path, bending R and then L, to pass over a small stream in a gully. Close to the first waterfall (Rhaeadr Fach), cross over a stile, then a wooden bridge to continue on with wall on R. **8.** At fence with stile, go over stile and then L, keeping fence on L and down, to cross Afon Rhaeadr Fawr by a wooden bridge. Up steps and L to kissing gate. Follow track, passing Nant Cottage (exhibition open Easter to October) and down to wooden gate. Through kissing gate and over bridge. L down road to junction. At minor road, North Wales Path goes R whilst Abergwyngregyn village and the Bont Newydd car park are L.

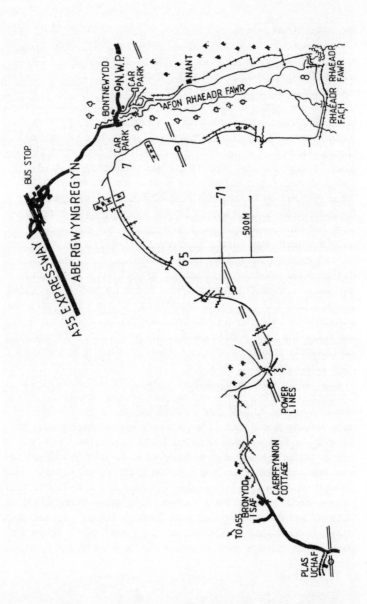

18

Refreshments: Plenty of eating places in Bangor, either cafes, restaurants or pubs serving good grub. Seasonal cafe in Abergwyngregyn mostly open at weekends and Bank holidays. The Aber Falls Hotel has had a chequered history, and in 1997 it was again refurbished at some expense and will survive hopefully. On our most recent visits, it has proved a very welcoming stop with good food and beers, well done!

Accommodation: Plenty of B and B's in Bangor especially around the Garth area, near to the pier. There is also a YHA hostel close to Porth Penrhyn. At Abergwyngregyn , there is a B and B at "The Vicarage" and "The Aber Falls Hotel".

Transport: Starting from Bangor Railway station to Porth Penrhyn adds 1½ miles/ 2.4 kilometres to the walk. Starting from Bangor bus station adds ½ mile/800 metres to the walk. From the finish of the walk at Bont Newydd to the bus stop in Abergwyngregyn village adds 1 mile/1.6 kilometres to the walk

Buses run from Bangor towards Abergwyngregyn every half hour (No 5 for Llandudno). Buses run from Abergwyngregyn towards Bangor every half hour (No 5 for Bangor). Phone 01286 679535 to confirm times of the services before setting out.

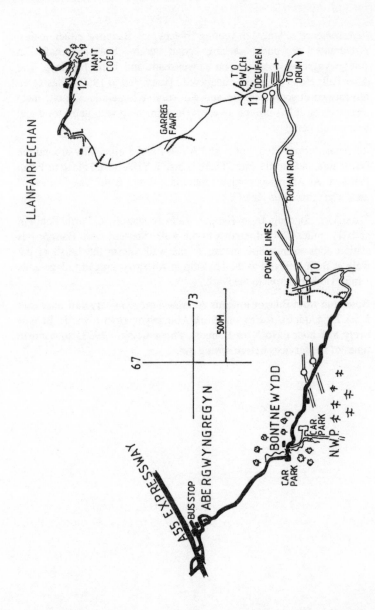

LLANFAIRFECHAN

NANT Y COED

12

GARREG FAWR

11

TO BWLCH Y DDEUFAEN

TO DRUM

ROMAN ROAD

POWER LINES

10

73

67

500M

ABERGWYNGREGYN

BONTNEWYDD

9

BUS STOP

A55 EXPRESSWAY

CAR PARK

CAR PARK

N.W.P.

Abergwyngregyn to Penmaenmawr (to leave the North Wales path at Bryn Derwydd)

Maps	1:50,000 Landranger sheet 115 Caernarfon and Bangor; or 1:25,000 Outdoor Leisure sheet 17 Snowdon and Conwy.
Distance	7.5miles/12 kilometres to Bryn Derwydd. To the car park near the entrance to Craiglwyd Caravan Park, 10miles/16 kilometres.
Height gained	Up to Carreg Fawr 1249ft/381metres and up to Meini Hirion (*Druids circle*) 1226ft/374metres.
Duration	5½ hours.
Terrain	Mostly on good dry tracks.
Car Park	For the walk start, park at Bont Newydd G.R.662720.

For the walk finish, park near entrance to Craiglwyd Caravan Park in Penmaenmawr G.R. 721759.

Abergwyngregyn was the seat of one of the main courts of the princes of Gwynedd. The exact location of Llywelyn's court at Aber is a matter of dispute. A strong contender is the 17th century house at Pen-y-bryn – much old structure still stands on the site, including a barn with massive stonework and slit windows which are, it is said, the oldest in Wales. Also at Aber is a Norman motte-and-bailey castle known as Pen y Mwd – it is a round twenty-two foot high earthwork close to the river and was probably built by Hugh Avranches, the Norman earl of Chester, during the period immediately preceeding Llywelyn's era. The site itself is on a private land and permission for access will be required from Ty'n-y-mwd.

Abergwyngregyn was also an important destination for travellers. An ancient route extended from here towards the Ynys Môn shore across Traeth Lafan, and was in use until the 19th century. Coaches and horses would travel across the sands to meet a ferry that took passengers on to Beaumaris on Ynys Môn. The bells of the church in

Abergwyngregyn would have acted as a guide for those travellers returning in bad weather.

The road from Bont Newydd climbs steadily to meet the track which was once a Roman road joining the garrison at Segontium (Caernarfon) with the one at Canovium (Caerhun) in the Conwy valley. For those feeling energetic, when you leave track, it is possible to continue on to Bwlch y Ddeufaen (G.R.715717). This remote and quiet pass has two large standing stones either side of the road, and close by is the large capped grave known as Barclodiad y Gawres.

As the path descends towards the village of Llanfairfechan, take a look out towards the sea. The area of sand hereabouts is steeped in Welsh legend. It tells of a 6th century kingdom known as Helig where there were once great cities and lush meadows, now drowned and lying under the sea in an area noted on O.S. Maps as Dutchman Bank. More recently this area was also the site of a tragic shipwreck. On the 17th of August 1831 the paddle steamer "The Rothsay Castle" was wrecked, resulting in the loss of one hundred and thirty of her one hundred and fifty passengers. It was recorded that the vessel was in a most unseaworthy condition and that, during the journey from the River Mersey towards the Menai Straits, the Master was drinking very heavily. Ignoring the crews requests to turn back from the teeth of a rising gale, she ran aground on the sand banks close to Llanfairfechan. One passenger realising that he was close to land tied himself into a barrel and, with a discarded umbrella, launched himself into the sea. After unfurling the brolly, he used it as a sail to take him safely to shore. One lady, having been dragged onto a makeshift raft, was faced with the indignity of a hushed argument amongst her male companions. When she asked to be included in the discussion, she was informed by a rather embarrassed spokesman that, as the raft was being swept out to sea, they needed her skirt to make a makeshift sail. The lady not only consented to this, but for the spokesman's bravery in asking, gave him her garter. Holding the skirt before them, and with the lady in her bloomers and waving a handkerchief as a distress signal, the raft sailed on until they were rescued by the Beaumaris lifeboat.

Leaving Llanfairfechan the path now climbs the flanks of Penmaenmawr. This area contains many ancient relics, perhaps the chief of these being the outpost of Braich y Ddinas, which stands on the conical peak of Dinas Penmaen. The fort consists of a number of hut circles contained within a loose stone wall of some height and thickness. This outpost is considered by some experts as one of the strongest and most defensible hill-forts in north-western Wales. One of the largest prehistoric axe factories to be found in the United Kingdom was discovered in 1919 on the flanks of Craiglwyd (G.R.717749).

Close to the summit of Moelfre is Meini Hirion. Long associated with the two sinister goddesses Andras and Ceridwen, the site is marked by ten upright stones set in a small circle, with smaller stones set in between. Perhaps connected with religious ceremonies or maybe marking the grave of some great hero, the site is a highlight in an area full of historical importance.

The base of Moelfre saw the tragic loss of the B24 Liberator bomber "Bachelors Baby" in early January 1944. On a flight from RAF Valley on Ynys Môn to Watton in East Anglia, the aircraft hit the top of Mynydd Bach whilst in low cloud and came to rest at the base of Moelfre, resulting in the loss of five of the eleven crew.

An attractive descent can be made by means of the Jubilee walk constructed in 1888 to commemorate the jubilee of Queen Victoria in 1887. This passes around Moel Lus and here the walker can look down on to the crowded coastal plain, with the sprawling village of Penmaenmawr, the expressway, and the railway all jostling for space at this narrow point.

Walk 9. For those continuing the walk from Aber Falls, at Bont Newydd R up road to top car park. For those starting from Abergwyngregyn village L over bridge at Bont Newydd and up road to top car park. R through car park and pass through field gate. Continue up along track. **10.** By first pylon (on L close to wall with wall stile) go R, track now runs parallel to power lines. Follow this to road crest. **11.** 75 metres after crest (opposite track to Drum) L, passing close to large pylon. At wall corner continue on along middle track, now grassy. At next track junction, ½ L downhill to wall corner. When wall

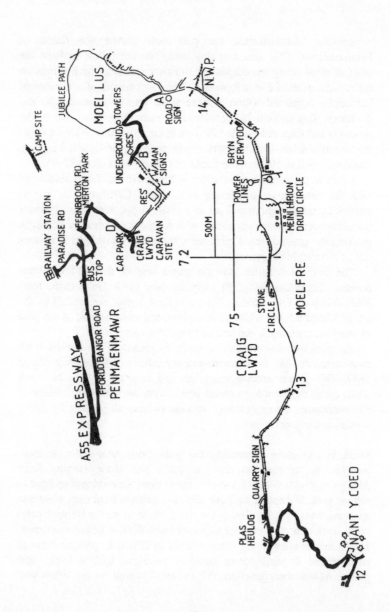

24

starts to bear L, continue on downhill (towards Ynys Seiriol). At wall, pass through kissing gate and ½ R down field. At sharp L hand bend, take the path continuing straight on to stile. Over stile, and path continues to descend between old wall and fence. Over next stile and cross field to kissing gate; go through this and onto road. **12.** R along road and, at fork in road, continue along R up hill. At next fork L down track to bridge over stream. Cross this and continue on up road (sign for Nant-y-coed on R). At crest of hill, sharp R (close to entrance to Plas Heulog) and continue on along road. At sharp L hand bend (ARC Northern Quarry sign), R to pass through gate and along track to farm (Blaen Llwyn). Through farm yard and next gate, continuing along rough track with fence and old wall on R. **13.** Final gate leads to open moorland, and continue along gradually ascending grassy track. Later, path runs close to wall. After 50 metres path bears away from the wall. As the North Wales Path descends to L, continue on grassy track for 100 metres. Take small path ½ R towards ridge crest, passing hut circles and the Druid circle of Meini Hirion. Path then descends to small gully and crosses stream. Path now rejoins North Wales Path. R along track which soon runs with wall on R. R passing through gate and down to a line of trees. L along track passing Bryn Derwydd cottage. Continue along track through gate. **14.** At gate on R go R to continue on North Wales Path. **At this point those wishing to carry on along the North Wales Path will need to turn to the next chapter. Those who have parked a car in Penmaenmawr, or are using public transport to make a return, should continue with the directions below. A.** At gate on R continue along track. 40 metres after 'No Entry' sign, R along track to a final wall corner. Here continue on grassy path which later descends to a bench (track junctions). On along the level path on L, contouring around the flanks of Moel Lus to pass between two towers. R down Mountain Road. **B.** At under ground water tank, L through kissing gate keeping fence on R. Follow walking man posts. **C.** At dip in track, opposite reservoir boundary, R over stile. Path now skirts reservoir boundary. Continue down road to entrance to Craiglwyd Caravan Park and car park. **D.** To continue into Penmaenmawr R, then L down Merton Park. L down Fernbrook Road to the Main road (Ffordd Bangor). Here the bus stop is on the left. For the railway station, cross main road and down Paradise Road.

Refreshments: Penmaenmawr is rather short on cafes, though the Mountain View pub is handy for bar snacks and accommodation. In Capelulo the cafe, Y Bedol Fach is very pleasant.

Accommodation: There are some B and B's in Penmaenmawr including the Mountain View public house, also Plas Heulog offers accommodation for walkers. Camp site at Trwyn-y-wylfa (close to Moel Lus) at G.R. 729769.

Transport: Starting from the bus stop in Abergwyngregyn will add 1mile/1.6 kilometres to the walk. From the finish of the walk near Craiglwyd Caravan Park to the bus stop and train station will add little more than ½ mile/800 metres for those reliant on public transport. Buses (bus no 5) run back to Abergwyngregyn every half hour. Phone 01286 679535 to confirm times. The train service will take you to Bangor or Conwy, check with the relevant authority for times.

Penmaenmawr to Conwy

Maps	1:50,000 Landranger sheet 115 Bangor and Caernarfon; or 1:25,000 Outdoor Leisure sheet 17 Snowdon and Conwy.
Distance:	6 miles/9.6 kilometres.
Height gained:	1226ft/374 metres to the *Druids Circle*.
Duration:	4 hours.
Terrain:	Paths mostly good and dry, one wet patch coming up from Penmaenmawr.
Car Park:	For the start of the walk, a small parking area close to Craiglwyd Caravan Park at G.R.721759. If parking in Conwy, various pay and display car parks. If arriving by train to start the walk, go up Paradise Road and cross the main road (Ffordd Bangor). Up Fernbrook Road and R up Merton Park to T-junction. R along Craiglwyd Road. From bus stop, as above from Ffordd Bangor.

Those joining the North Wales Path from Penmaenmawr will find the path from Craiglwyd Farm (kennels) to be slightly steep but most enjoyable. The footpath follows the signs for the Druids Circle, Meini Hirion. On regaining the North Wales Path, a short diversion can be made to visit this Bronze age site and the nearby Neolithic axe factory on Craiglwyd. The North Wales Path now crosses open moorland, with good views of Tal-y-fan. Later the path meanders down to the tree lined Pen Sychnant or Sychnant Pass. Cross the road and head up to explore the prehistoric hill-fort of Castell Seion on the summit of Mynydd Conwy. This stone walled hill fort now consists of about fifty stone huts and levelled house platforms, whilst at the western end, the remains of a Keep can be found. The North Wales Path runs just below the ridge, but a worthwhile alternative would be to walk the ridge heading in the direction of Conwy.

Conwy has a long and fascinating history. For those who wish to know more, the time taken to do the walk should allow plenty of time later in the day for exploration.

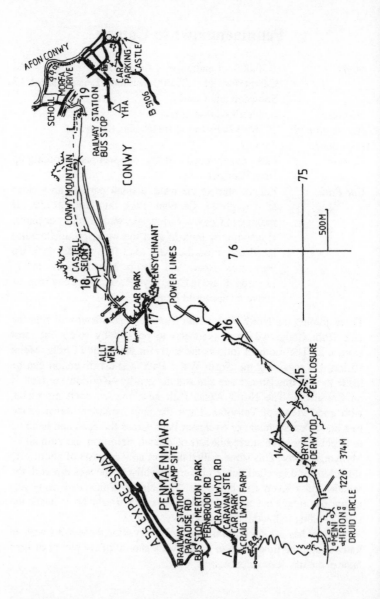

28

The town first came to prominence in 1185, when an Order of Cistercian monks established an Abbey here. The great Welsh Prince Llywelyn ap Iorwerth (Llywelyn Fawr) gave his blessing to the Order and bestowed upon it an endowment from the land he owned in Caernarfon, Denbigh and Ynys Môn. He granted privileges and exemptions for the Abbey, including a right to all shipwrecks in the area and free passage over a number of rivers. On his death in 1240 Llywelyn ap Iorwerth was laid to rest in the Abbey, but later, on the succession of Edward, the Cistercian order of Monks was moved to Maenan, near Llanrwst, bearing the coffin of Llywelyn ap Iorwerth with them. Thus Edward cleared the way for his Castle and fortified town to be built on the site that was previously occupied by the Abbey.

The construction of Edward's "Iron Ring" of fortresses was one of Europe's most ambitious medieval building projects. Construction of Conwy Castle started in 1283 and took only four years to complete. Built under the watchful eye of the master military architect, James of St George d'Esperance and with a workforce of some fifteen hundred men, it is estimated that at today's prices the Castle would have cost four and a half million pounds. The Castle here in Conwy was based on a principle Edward had seen used in castles in Gascony in south-west France, where Edward was a Duke. During the day the local people were permitted to enter the town, but could not trade or carry weapons. However at night the gates to the town were shut and only the English families were allowed to stay within the protected walls. These walls themselves make a fine walk and, if time allows, they give an unique view of the town.

Despite its formidable appearance the Castle did succumb to attack. On Good Friday in 1401, during the rebellion led by Owain Glyndŵr, the Castle was successfully occupied by Gwylym and Rhys ap Tudur. (They were members of the Ynys Môn family who were later to produce the Tudor Dynasty). The Castle was taken by surprise whilst the garrison of thirty men were in Church. Forty-five Welsh rebels, headed by the Tudors, entered the Castle and took control.

Following the rebellion by Owain Glyndŵr the Castle fell into a state of disrepair. In March 1627, Charles sold the Castle to Lord Conwy for the sum of one hundred pounds. The Castle was now in such a state of dereliction that it could not be safely entered. However, its days of military importance had not ended. In 1646 on the breakout of Civil War, it was repaired and re-garrisoned for the Royalists by locally born John Williams (archbishop of York), who was then one of Charles' most loyal supporters. In 1646 the castle was besieged by the Parliamentarians, under the command of General Mytton, and after a siege lasting three months the Royalists surrendered to the General.

After the Civil War all fortifications were rendered unusable and the process of decline began. Indeed, so much of the Castle had become militarily useless that in 1665, the grandson of Lord Conwy, "under the pretence of work being done for his Majesty's service" stripped the Castle of its lead, ironwork and timber, and had it shipped out to Ireland to sell.

Walk A. At Craiglwyd Farm (kennels) and sign for Druids Circle, L up to farm; continue up with fence on L and buildings on R. At rear of buildings, a small sign for the Druids Circle can be found close to a kissing gate. Through the gate, with the path climbing to the L. Continue upwards passing a number of benches. Over bridge and up to kissing gate in wall. Go through kissing gate and R, following wall to regain the track for the North Wales Path. Here a diversion can be made to Meini Hirion by crossing the track and heading uphill. The North Wales Path goes L along track. *B.* Track soon runs close to wall on R. Later, R through gate, and down to line of trees, then L along track passing "Bryn Derwydd" Cottage. Continue along track through gate. **14.** At gate on R, go R onto moorland then ½L towards wall passing under powerlines. At track junction, R down to stream, cross wall and bridge. Continue up to L/Hand and corner of enclosure. Carry on up with wall on R. **15.** Close to trees by ruin in enclosure, go L on path rising through bracken. Later, path runs along with wall on L. Track continues on away from wall, to join track from the right (vehicle track). Go L along track, running parallel to powerlines. **16.** At R/Hand bend in track onwards over stile. Path now meanders down to a line of trees. At wall with trees behind, L to gate. Go through gate and down to road. **17.** Cross road and along track, passing under overhanging rock. Track sweeps up to L. 150 metres before farm, go R over stream using stepping stones (footpath sign nearby), and passing under powerlines. At crossing track continue on sweeping to R to join track from L. **18.** When track levels out, go R towards wall and powerlines. *At this point instead of heading towards the wall and power lines continue on upwards and to the ridge line to explore the fort. The ridge descends gradually in the direction of the town of Conwy. Continue down to wall, and continue with wall on L, following wall around to R, passing over stile and between houses and down to road.* At path junction, cross this and bear L. The path now runs level, crossing over next junction to meet a broader path from R. Now along the flanks of Mynydd Conwy passing close to the prehistoric hill fort of Castell Seion. After descending path from the fort joins the main track, the track narrows and starts to descend. Close to tree on L continue descent to an area of rock slabs close to path. Here cross junction and continue descending through slightly wooded area and down to stile. *At this point the alternative also joins the road.* Continue down road to junction taking the L fork. **19.** Continue along road and over railway footbridge. Cross main road and continue along Morfa Drive to school. At the end of school property, go R along tarmac footpath running close to estuary. At end of footpath, turn L under castle wall and along Quay.

Refreshments Good refreshments to be had in Conwy, especially Anna's above the Climbing Shop in the High Street. The Wall Place is also highly recommended, serving interesting vegetarian food off Chapel Street, very near to the town walls. Plenty of fish and chip shops as well as the Liverpool Arms on the Quay where you can sit outside and watch the world go by.

Accommodation There is a campsite on the Trefriw road out of Conwy. YHA on the road to Sychnant Pass at GR 775775 (Lark Hill Tel. 01492 593571). Otherwise, some B and B's and hotels in Conwy itself.

Transport There is a train station in Conwy for those wishing to return to Penmaenmawr but not all trains stop at these stations. Bus stop in the town square of Conwy for buses towards Bangor (including

Penmaenmawr). Bus stop in Conwy town's main street, for buses to Llandudno. Both bus no 5. For bus enquiries telephone 01286 679535 or 01492 575410.

Conwy to Llandudno

Maps: 1:50,000 Landranger sheet 115 Bangor and
      Caernarfon or 1:25,000 Outdoor Leisure sheet 17
      Snowdon and Conwy.

Distance: 8 miles/12.8 kilometres

Height gained: 300ft/91 metres

Duration: 4½ hours

Terrain: Virtually all on road except for the area close to the
      golf course, where the walking is through sand
      dunes.

Car Park: There are numerous pay and display car parks in
      Conwy, although free car parking is more difficult to
      come by. The situation is similar in Llandudno
      although the area around the Tram Station may be
      worth a try for free parking.

This walk leaves the picturesque quay in Conwy and heads towards one of the towns most important features. Conwy has always been important as a crossing point for Afon Conwy, and now there are two road bridges and a railway bridge providing a link (plus a tunnel). Conwy has not always been as easy to reach by road. This changed in the early 19th century when a bridge replaced the dangerous and inefficient ferry. In 1802, an engineer named John Rennie proposed to span the estuary by means of a vast high level bridge, but his plans had the bridge passing right through the castle, and were ultimately rejected in favour of those put forward by Thomas Telford. Telford's design was for a graceful suspension bridge with mock medieval towers. The bridge was opened in 1826 and remained in service as a toll bridge until the opening of the larger new bridge in December 1958. The railway bridge was built by Robert Stephenson in 1840, and represented a tremendous technical achievement for its time. This bridge was a vital link in the completion of the Chester to Holyhead Railway and the subsequent development of Holyhead as a major ferry port. The bridge consisted of two rectangular iron tubes, four hundred and twenty four feet long and weighing thirteen hundred tons, each of

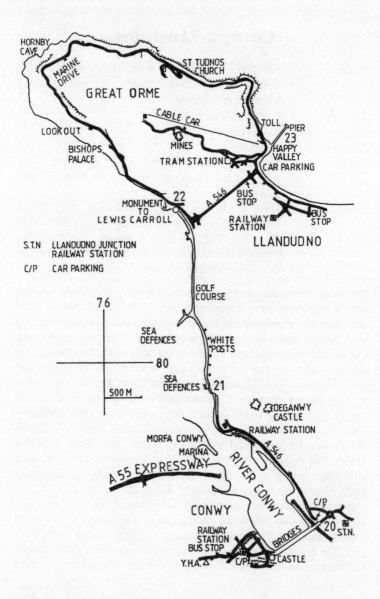

which were supported by towers (not unlike those on Telfords bridge) with mock medieval details to blend in with the Castle. These tubes were assembled near the site and floated into position on huge rafts. It's ironic to think that just over one hundred and fifty years after the complex construction of the railway bridge, a very similar system was used to construct the road tunnel for the Expressway. A large basin was dug out and four tubes, rectangular in section, were constructed within this basin. In the estuary the river bed was dredged in order to provide a firm base. The tube ends were then blanked off and the basin breached, the tubes were floated into position, bolted together and then sunk into the dredged channel. With the ends of the tunnel linked to the access roads, the tunnel was opened by Queen Elizabeth II on the 5th of October 1991. The basin where the tubes were constructed is now a thriving marina.

The quay at Conwy was also famous for its shellfish and for those who enjoy cockles and mussels, Keith the Fish can still be found selling locally caught produce on the quay itself. Although oysters are still sold from his van it is unlikely that you will be lucky enough to find within them the fresh water pearls for which the estuary was famous. A particularly fine example was presented to Queen Catherine, the wife of Charles II by Robert Wynne of Castell Gwydir near Llanrwst. The pearl was supposed to have been given place of honour in her Royal Crown.

The empty mussel shells from the mussel industry in the estuary were thrown onto a heap at Morfa Conwy (where the golf course is today) and in time grew to such a sizeable mound that it formed a land mark for mariners entering the river. It seems that the market for shellfish in this country has declined, and the once thriving industry now sells its limited catch abroad.

No rivers are without their tales and legends and the one surrounding Afon Conwy is the tale of an unfortunate Mermaid who was caught by local fishermen. After hauling her into their boat and transporting her to Conwy they allowed her to suffocate in the air. For some reason the local fishermen believed she was responsible for the loss of mariners in the district. She died cursing the fishermen of Conwy, vowing that many of them would perish at sea and that disasters would befall the town. It is claimed that she died on the site of the old Town hall, and when it was raised to the ground by fire, some locals thought they heard the Mermaid's ghostly laughter. A civic hall built on the same spot suffered a similar fate and was burnt to the ground only two months after its completion. Again, strange laughter was heard at the time of the fire!

The walk now follows the estuary with fine views of the most northerly ridges of the Snowdonia range, as well as the small but significant Mynydd Deganwy.

On approaching Llandudno's West Shore, look out for a statue depicting characters from the Lewis Carroll book *Alice's Adventures in Wonderland*. The statue, by F W Forrester, was inspired by the work of Lewis Carroll, and was dedicated by David Lloyd George M.P. in 1933. Lewis Carroll, whose real name was the Reverend Charles Ludwidge Dodgson was a lecturer in mathematics at Oxford University. It is claimed that he often came to Llandudno with his friend and colleague Henry Liddell, who had a holiday home here. The holiday home is now the Gogarth Abbey Hotel. It is also claimed that the stories were told to Alice Liddell, the young daughter of Henry Liddell, during strolls along the sands in the company of Rev Dodgson. Dodgson later decided to write these stories down and they were given to Alice as a Christmas present. In 1871 Dodgson wrote a follow up, "Through the Looking Glass and what Alice found there", under the pen name of Lewis Carroll. Sadly the statue has been vandalised and, in order to protect it from further damage, it has been surrounded by metal bars. There is very considerable doubt that Dodgson ever set foot in Llandudno, and actually wrote the stories for Alice Liddell following boating trips on the Thames at Oxford.

The Walk Leave the quay at Conwy and ascend to the road bridge. Go L crossing the bridge and passing through the gardens. At end of gardens, up ramp passing over Expressway. **20.** Down steps underneath large road sign (close to bus depot). Go L along road which soon joins main road, A546. L along pavements to Deganwy Railway Station car park. At end of car park, L down Marine Crescent, crossing railway lines. At road end continue on along Promenade. At the end of the Promenade, continue along top of beach to wooden sea defences. **21.** At wooden sea defences, R into dunes to edge of golf course. Path follows a line of white posts. At large patch of gorse, keep close to top of beach passing close to another set of sea defences. Continue along path to reach car park. After car park, join the promenade and continue along this to reach a paddling pool. **22.** By this pool the monument to Lewis Carroll will be found; after this return to promenade. Shortly, join the road and go L up Marine Drive, passing old toll house on R. Continue along Marine Drive passing access to old Lighthouse (now a wonderfully positioned Bed and Breakfast) and later the access to the St Tudno's Church. Continue on to pass another toll house (this time in use) and onto the access to the Pier. **23.** The walk now follows the Promenade, finishing at an Obelisk.

Refreshments The choice in Llandudno should cater for any appetite, the closest cafe to the end of the walk is the Habit Tea Rooms, which can be recommended. Otherwise Llandudno is not short on cafes, take your pick.

Accommodation Plenty of B and B's to chose from, especially around the Tram Station at the Pier end of the town. Those wishing for somewhere more unusual could return to the Old Lighthouse passed on the Marine Drive.

Transport Buses run from Llandudno to Bangor, Conwy, Rhyl and Deganwy. For Bangor to Llandudno the bus stop is in Castle St, bus No5 from stop R. For Llysfaen, Llandudno *via* Deganwy, catch the bus No15 from the stop in Lancaster Square. For those going in the Rhyl direction, bus No16 goes from a stop in Lancaster Square. Railway travellers can catch a train from Llandudno to Llandudno Junction, where they will need to change but note that not all trains from the Junction towards Bangor stop in Conwy. For timetable enquiries phone 01286 679535 or 01492 575410.

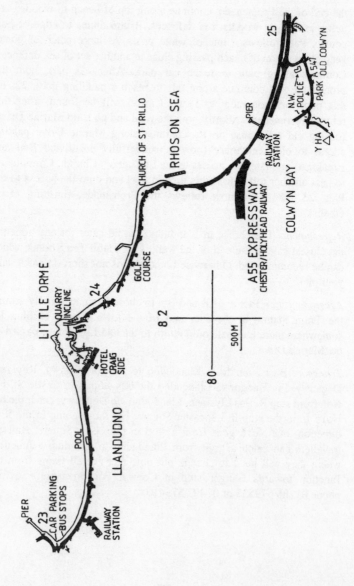

PIER

23

CAR PARKING
BUS STOPS

RAILWAY
STATION

LLANDUDNO

POOL

HOTEL
CRAIG
SIDE

LITTLE ORME

QUARRY
INCLINE

24

GOLF COURSE

CHURCH OF ST TRILLO

RHOS ON SEA

PIER

RAILWAY
STATION

A55 EXPRESSWAY
CHESTER/HOLYHEAD RAILWAY

COLWYN BAY

25

N.W.
POLICE

PARK A547 OLD COLWYN

Y HA

500M

8 2

80

Llandudno to Llysfaen

Maps:	1:50,000 Landranger sheet 115 Bangor and Caernarfon, Landranger sheet 116 Denbigh and Colwyn Bay; or 1:25,000 Outdoor Leisure sheet 17 Snowdon and Conwy.
Distance:	9¾miles/15.6 kilometres
Height gained:	650ft/200metres.
Duration:	4½ hours.
Terrain:	Initially road walking and along promenades but later through agricultural land, which may be muddy.
Car Park:	At the pier end of Llandudno, parking can be found in the side streets around the Tram Station but check how long you can stay. At Llysfaen there is a good car park close to the Castle Inn, but avoid parking close to the cliffs as these are used by rock climbers, G.R.887775. To locate the Castle Inn, drive out of Colwyn Bay on the A547 towards Abergele. After passing the Colwyn Bay Hotel (known locally as Hotel 70 Degrees), take the turning R, uphill for Llysfaen. Go up Highlands Road for approximately 1 mile (1.6 kilometres), looking for a minor turning on R, Tan y Graig Road. Follow this to the Castle Inn.

This next section of the North Wales Path runs along the Victorian Promenades of the most popular tourist areas of the North Wales coast. The start point for the walk is Llandudno, the name deriving from that of St Tudno. However the town was not really developed until much later in its history. Edward Mostyn, who was a local land owner and MP for the area, realised that there was a growing passion for sea bathing and thinking this could be exploited, he set about creating a spectacular resort for the Middle classes. He was able to force an enclosure act through Parliament, giving him right to the land in the area. This was accomplished through the help of the Bishop of

Bangor who was thought to be in the pocket of Edward Mostyn. Work started in about 1850 under the watchful eye of Owain Williams, a Liverpool surveyor. The resort gained popularity and rapidly became the premier destination for those Victorians seeking sophistication. Popular music stars of the day such as Adelia Patti and the French conductor Jules Rivere were amongst many to play at the town. The latter was famous for sitting in a gilded chair with his back to the musicians, conducting with a bejewelled ivory baton. Mostyn Street, the main street with its wrought iron and glass verandas, was reputed to be the finest shopping area outside of London. The hotels in the resort were patronised by titled guests such as Napoleon the III, Disraeli, Gladstone and also the Queen of Romania, Queen Elizabeth (who came by mistake).

The grandeur from this previous age has not totally deserted the town, and it still has an air of splendour. The entertainment has changed somewhat although a Punch and Judy show still runs in the holiday season, close to the entrance to the Pier. Ringo Starr, the drummer with the 'The Beatles' once worked on the pleasure steamers which called at the pier on their North Wales cruises from Liverpool.

After the stroll along the 'Prom', the walk now branches on to the flanks of the Little Orme, whose limestone cliffs drop steeply for 400ft into the sea. Its summit commands spectacular views of the surrounding countryside. Later, the walk descends the inclines of long abandoned quarries to emerge once more on the coastal promenades.

This next section of coast has been associated with the legend of Prince Madog and his journey to discover the Americas some three hundred years before Columbus. Madog was born some time between 1134 and 1142 in Dolwyddelan Castle, and was one of Owain Gwynedd's nineteen children. He was a brother to Prince Idwal, after whom Llyn Idwal is named. His departure point has been located by historians as the mouth of Afon Ganol, in an area then known as Aber Cerrig Gwynion, believed to be the area now known as Llandrillo-yn-Rhos. Sea defences have been located in the rockery of the house known as Odstone, next to the golf course, which might date from the period when Madog sailed on his epic voyage. The estimated size of the sea defences would indicate that ships of up to thirty tons could have been built in the basin. What is known of ship building in the 12th century suggests that planked vessels were clad in a covering of tarred cow hide, as was the practice with the Irish Curraghs and the Welsh Corracle. It is likely that the craft had single masts with a single square sail. Legend claims that thirteen ships set sail with up to three hundred crew on this voyage of discovery, but it is more likely that just two vessels, *Gwennan Corn* (sailed by Madog) and *Pedr Sant* (sailed by Madog's brother, Rhyd) made the voyage. Madog is believed to have successfully landed in Mobile Bay in Alabama in 1170. The landing site is now marked by a memorial tablet placed there on 10th November 1953 by the Virginia Cavalier Chapter of the Daughters of the American Revolution, bearing the inscription,

In memory of Prince Madoc, the Welsh explorer
who landed on the shores of Mobile Bay in 1170
and left behind, with the Indians, the Welsh language.

Close to the area of Madog's departure is the tiny chapel of St Trillo. The original chapel was believed to have been built around the 6th Century and the present structure is only nine feet in height, with seating for twelve people. St Trillo was an early British hermit who built his cell on the site of a holy well at Llandrillo-yn-Rhos. Unfortunately over the years the cell and the adjoining well fell into disrepair until the Cistercian monks restored the cell in 1180. This enabled them to pray for a good haul of fish in the great weir, whose remains can still be seen on the foreshore at Rhos.

At the end of the promenade the path turns inland and follows Nant Ysgubor Newydd. On the left, above the river, can be seen a folly constructed by a Justice of Peace for the area, Sir Charles Woodhall. Sir Charles was addicted to his pipe and was forbidden to smoke in his own house, so he decided to build himself a retreat where he could smoke to his hearts content. In 1894, opposite his mansion of Tan-y-coed, he landscaped the hilly wooded area, and built a castle shaped folly. Here he could be king of his own small castle. On the death of Sir Charles, in 1926, the council opened the gardens and the folly to the public. This became a popular haunt for the tourists and locals alike but unfortunately as is all too often the case, the folly became a

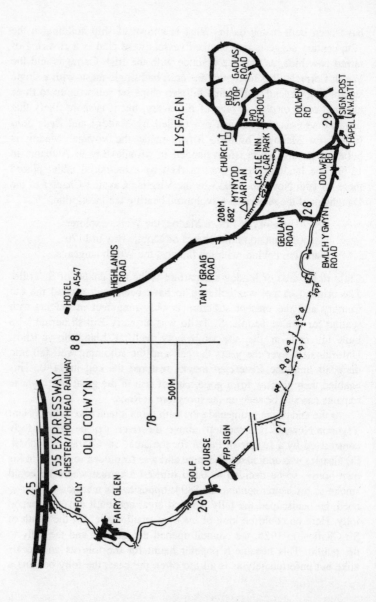

target for vandalism. Over the years it has been home to a number of organisations but, due to deterioration, it was eventually sold and converted into a residence.

Walk 23. The walk goes east, following the promenade from the pier, and later passing a childrens bathing pool, before joining the road. Continue up the hill to pass the Craig-side Inn on the R. Near the brow of the hill, a sign post will be seen by a field and kissing gate. Go L through the kissing gate and R along an ascending path, which rises to the R of a small crag. Close to the crag take a R fork through bushes, with fence on R. Through kissing gate, and continue with fence on R. Just before a craggy ridge, ½R towards fence with path running through an area of gorse, before rejoining the fence. Continue through gorse to quarry edge. Go R and soon descend L into shallow gully and onto plateau. Cross plateau to kissing gate, go through this and descend incline. Cross to fence and R following fence, dropping into a slight hollow before rising up to L to follow track. Just before houses, L down steps to road and R along road. **24.** Where road swings to R and with grassy area on L, go L along path and down steps to beach. R along top of beach and, just after houses, ascend steps to promenade. L along promenade passing St Trillo's church and Rhos-on-Sea. Later the promenade passes close to the Pier. **25.** At the end of the promenade, the road bends R passing under bridges; here go R following the pedestrian way with stream on R. Cross road to footpath and continue along with river on R. Look out for the folly on L. Path later passes under buildings. Continue on with stream on R and near end of paved area, go L up steps to road. Cross road to Fairy Glen road sign, and R along lane to river. Do not cross river but keep on with river on R. Where a metal bridge with hoops crosses the river, continue with river on R, later up to road. **26.** R along road for 100 metres, then L up path between houses (Greenlands) to stile. ½R crossing golf course towards white gate, passing through field gate close to white gate. Cross road and up track for 20 metres, then L over stile following field boundary on L. At end of field, over stile and L up lane to gate on R with footpath sign for Geulan Road. R over stile and down field, following grassy track. **27.** At field bottom corner L, keeping hedge on R to next corner, with stile in trees. Over stile and cross field to wood corner, not obvious at first, with North Wales Path sign. Follow vague level path in woods to fence with stile. Over stile and cross field to wall stile, over stile and along path in woods passing into next field. Cross this field to top corner (North Wales Path sign) and into woods taking the higher of two descending paths to a stile, close to stream. Over this and up field and over next stile, then ½R up to track. L up track to gate and pass through. At property called Pebi Gardens, go L along drive to road. **28.** R along Bwlch-y-gwynt Road, and at road junction go uphill, now Dolwen Road, to a major road junction. Here, up hill to pass Tabor Chapel and continue along Dolwen road. **29.** At North Wales Path and Bryn Defaid sign on R, terminate this section of the walk.

Refreshments The Castle Inn is a large pub close to the end of the walk providing bar meals and log fires, also seasonal cafes may be found.

Accommodation Little to offer in Llysfaen although it may be worth checking at the Post Office. Otherwise B and B's in Llandudno, with a YHA at Foxhill, Nant y Glyn. Also, Colwyn Bay is near at hand.

Transport In Llandudno the bus stops are situated near the junction of Mostyn St and Gloddaeth St. Whilst in Llysfaen the bus stop is in Gadlas Road with the bus stopping outside the Spar shop. (Bus no 15 terminates in Llysfaen, Bus no 16 continues on to Rhyl. For those walkers wishing to join public transport at Gadlas Road, continue along Dolwen Road to a turning R into Gadlas Road. Alternatively the walker can continue along Ffordd-y-llan to Highlands Road and the A547, where there is a bus stop on the junction corner. For timetable enquiries phone 01492 575410.

Those walkers with transport at the Castle Inn retrace your steps to Tabor Chapel and take R fork rising to T junction. Here, L to Castle Inn.

Llysfaen to Rhyl

Maps: 1:50,000 Landranger sheet 116 Denbigh and Colwyn Bay; or 1:25,000 Outdoor Leisure sheet 17 Snowdon and Conwy and Pathfinder series 754 Abergele.

Distance: 8 miles/12.8 kilometres.

Height gained: A descent is made from 656ft/200metres to sea level.

Duration: 4 hours.

Terrain: Good hard agricultural land at first, then beach tops and promenades.

Car Park: At Llysfaen there is a good car park close to the Castle Inn but avoid parking close to the cliffs as these are used by rock climbers, G.R. 887776. To locate the Castle Inn, drive out of Colwyn Bay on the A547, the road climbs passing the Colwyn Bay Hotel (known locally as the Hotel 70 Degrees), shortly afterwards a turning R for Llysfaen will be seen. For those travelling from the Rhyl direction, the turning on the L is on the brow of a long hill and is the second turning seen for Llysfaen. Turn up this road (Highlands Road) for approximately ½ mile (800 metres) then look for minor road turning on R (Tan-y-graig Road); follow this to the Castle Inn on L.

To start the walk from the Castle Inn car park, R out of car park and along road. At sharp L/Hand junction, L onto Geulan Road. This dips then rises to level area. Here L down Bwlch-y-gwynt Road (it is a continuation of Geulan Road). At next major dip and road junction, uphill, now on Dolwen Road to a large road junction. Here uphill to pass Tabor Chapel on R. Continue along Dolwen Road to the sign post for North Wales Path and Bryn Defaid. Now follow the instructions from **29.** Those starting the walk from the Gadlas Road bus stop, walk along Gadlas Road to a T junction. Then L down Dolwen Road; do not take the descending road to L, but continue along to sign for North Wales Path and Bryn Defaid.

If parking in Rhyl, over the bridge by the Foryd Harbour and at roundabout continue on along the A548 for 25 metres to pay and display car park on R.

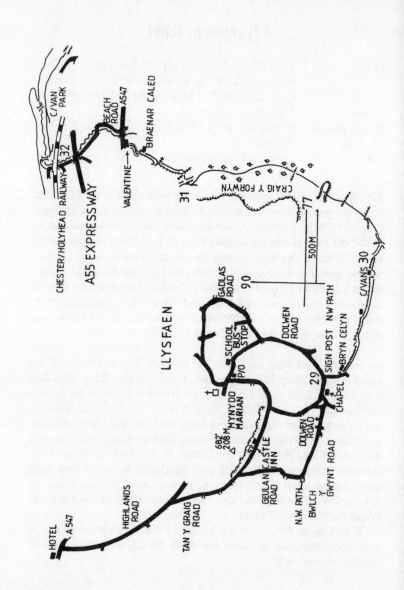

The footpath through Llysfaen contours around the flanks of Mynydd Marian and through the village, bypassing a vast limestone quarry and landfill site. Above the village is the escarpment known as the Castle Inn Quarry. This small crag is very popular with climbers, both for its easy access and its proximity to a pub, whilst later in the walk the more remote crag of Craig-y-forwyn is passed.

The footpath now returns to the coast and close by can be seen Castell Gwrych. This was built as a folly by the Duke of Dundonald in 1814, and was once earmarked as a possible residence for the Prince of Wales. Later the castle was turned into a holiday centre and amongst its many attractions were medieval jousting and banquets. The property was purchased in 1990 by a Californian property developer who wished to create a flamboyant five star hotel and a £10 million opera house dedicated to the late Richard Burton, who was never an opera singer! This project never saw the light of day. The property has now fallen into decay and has been taken over by a group of new age travellers.

The area of the coast through which the walk now passes is a Mecca for holiday makers, especially from the Merseyside and Midlands areas. This has resulted in a large number of caravan sites. Despite the increase in those taking foreign holidays, the area still retains its popularity.

If the view of caravan sites becomes too much, then look out to sea and try to picture the events from one day in 1939. On the 1st of June in that year, fifteen miles off the North Wales coast, His Majesty's Submarine, the 'Thetis' sank, with the loss of ninety-nine crew members. 'Thetis' was a T class patrol type submarine, built at Cammell Lairds shipyard in Birkenhead for general Navy service at the cost of some £350,000. Her displacement was approximately fifteen hundred tons with a length of two hundred and twenty feet, a beam of twenty-six feet and a depth of twelve feet. The normal ships compliment was fifty three officers and men. She was launched on the 29th of April 1938, for fitting out and initial sea trials. However, after a problematic series of trials in the Clyde estuary, she was returned to Cammell Lairds for the defects to be ironed out. On the 1st of June at 09.30 she slipped out of the basin for her final sea trials but on this day, observers and construction staff swelled the numbers on board to one hundred and three. At 13.30 the "Thetis" reached her dive position off the North Wales coast. The safety boat accompanying the submarine had suspicions of problems due to the huge amount of air bubbles coming from the bow of the "Thetis". After diving, the submarine never resurfaced again and sadly ninety-nine crew members perished from asphyxia and carbon monoxide poisoning. The four who survived managed to escape through the submarine's emergency hatch, and floated to the surface. Why more crew did not manage to leave the vessel by this method is a mystery, but the complexities of the escape mechanism may have proved too difficult to those already confused and bewildered from lack of oxygen.

The cause of the loss of the 'Thetis', was discovered after the vessel was finally refloated. During the refit, the glass sight ports for the torpedo tube had been painted over. On the tragic day, the operator, used to be being able to see into the tubes, assumed that the tube was empty and inadvertently opened the torpedo tube door. Being open to the sea this allowed the bow section to flood, causing the craft to dive steeply. The account of what happened on the surface was a pathetic tale of bad management and a failure to realise the seriousness of the situation. Her exact position was not discovered until the following morning when her stern was seen protruding out of the water. Even then there was a reluctance to approach the stricken craft, as the propeller was still revolving and may have injured any survivors. When the rescue craft did approach at 8.00a.m. that day, divers tried to attract attention by taping on the hull. Unfortunately there was no response.

With extreme difficulty, she was brought to the shallow shore at Traeth Bychan on Anglesey's east coastline, where she was beached, sealed and refloated. Some of the bodies were removed in Moelfre whilst the remainder were taken ashore at Holyhead. Every year since the disaster, a commemorative service has been held at the mass grave on the first Sunday in June.

The 'Thetis' was eventually repaired at Cammell Lairds yards and returned to service after being renamed the "Thunderbolt". She was engaged in convoy duties in the Mediterranean where she did excellent work. However the sad history of this vessel had not finished and on the 2nd of June 1943, just 4 years and 1 day after the Liverpool Bay fiasco, the London Gazette carried an Admiralty communiqué which read, "The Admiralty regrets to announce that His Majesty's Submarine 'Thunderbolt' must now be considered lost". She went down with all hands whilst attacking an Italian convoy bound for North Africa.

Between Abergele and Rhyl is the low lying area of Towyn, which between the 26th of February and the 2nd of March 1990, was subjected to several days of sustained south-westerly gales and storm force winds. This had the effect of raising the level of the tides. Continuous heavy rain had swollen the rivers, and this combination led to flood alerts being issued for the area. Despite these warnings, no one was prepared for what was to follow. On the 26th of February the wind went to the north and increased to force eleven (known as a violent storm). For a short time, force twelve or hurricane force winds were recorded. This wind, coupled with the low pressure, high tide and rough seas, breached the sea defences at Towyn and, because Afon Clwyd was swollen and overflowing from heavy rains, the consequence was severe flooding of Towyn and the surrounding low lying areas. The largest ever peace time evacuation in the United Kingdom took place, forcing over two thousand people to leave their homes. All the emergency services were drafted in to help including Coastguard rescue teams, the RNLI, RAF rescue helicopters as well as the Police and Fire Services. Social Services and the WRVS gave help and temporary accommodation to ease the plight of the unfortunate. Since that time much work has been done to improve the sea defences in the area.

Walk 29. R along track and, just after boundary wall for Bryn Celyn, go L over stile and into field. Along with large wall on L. At wall end, continue with fence on L passing close to cottages and then passing close to caravan site. Over stile and pass close to a stable. **30.** Continue on with fence on L. Over second stile and R down lane; where track bears to R, go L over stile and along grassy track until a wall corner, on the L, becomes visible. Up to this and over stile.

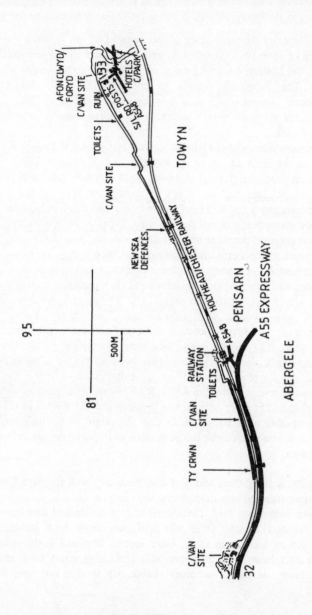

50

Continue to top of bank and over crest to stile over wall. Over this and cross field, heading towards ridge crest with sea behind. Path, faint at first, heads down into wood and runs along the base of screes (large crag above). **31.** At junction with road, sharp R down road for 5 metres, then L over stile and into field. Down field to next stile and over this. Go L down some concrete steps and along field with hedge on L, to gate with stile. Continue on to kissing gate, through this and down drive towards white house (Braenar Caled). ½L down enclosed path to pass under building, (The Valentine public house). Cross road, (A547) and R over bridge. At road junction, L down Beach Road crossing river and passing picnic area to join road, then R passing under bridges to shoreline. **32.** R along shore to bridge. Over bridge, then L with stream on L. Path now runs along top of beach to pass close to caravan site. Keep close to top of beach to join path rising above shingle. Path now runs parallel to road and railway to join a minor road just before next caravan site (Ty-crwn cottage at the start of this site). Follow road, passing caravan site, to car park with kiosks and toilets. Alternatively, at caravan site, walk along top of beach to reach kiosks and toilets. Continue to end of promenade dropping down to beach, and continuing along with railway on R. Up concrete ramp to footpath, running along with fence and wall, and parallel to railway on R. Path later drops again to top of beach to gain new concrete sea defences with path running along top. Later path crosses to run in front of caravan site and to pass close to area of dunes. After passing toilets and car park on R, pass derelict property. 45 metres before next caravan site, go R at gap in dunes and cross open ground, close to two blue posts. Through gap in fence and past estate of bungalows, (Southlands Road) to main road, A548. L after passing 'The Ferry' and cross bridge. **33.** Pass roundabout and under large road sign, then R to edge of lake.

Refreshments Both 'The Ferry' and 'The Harbour' are conveniently close to the end of the walk and both offer pub grub. On the way, 'The Valentines' is an old fashioned pub whose lure may be difficult to resist.

Accommodation There are many B and B's in Rhyl itself and, in order to be sure of the quality, it is probably best to book though the tourist information office.

Transport In Llysfaen the bus stop is situated in Gadlas Road (near the Spar shop) for Bus No 16 to Rhyl. In Rhyl there is a bus stop situated along the road to Abergele, about 100metres from 'The Ferry' and 'The Harbour', again Bus No 16. For timetable enquiries phone 01492 575410.

Rhyl to Prestatyn via Rhuddlan and Dyserth

Maps: 1:50,000 Landranger sheet 116 Denbigh and Colwyn Bay; or 1:25,000 Pathfinder sheet 737 Rhyl and 755 Holywell and St Asaph.

Distance: 9¼miles/15kilometres.

Height gained: 144ft/44metres.

Duration: 4½ hours.

Terrain: Mostly agricultural land, mainly dry except between the farms of Aberkinsey and Llewenllyd where a hedged bridleway may be muddy and wet.

Car Park: At Rhyl near to the bridge by the Foryd Harbour is a pay and display car park, G.R.996806. In Prestatyn, at the traffic lights on the A548, turn at sign for station, over railway bridge and first L. At next junction L, and close to Public house, L again to pay and display car park.

Before the 1800's, Rhyl was just a few fisherman's cottages clustered around the mouth of Afon Clwyd. At that time the area was known as Y Foryd, a name still used when referring to the river entrance. However the railway boom in 1840's brought the workers and families from the industrial towns of the North-West and Midlands of England to sample the sea air. The town grew, and amusement arcades and fun fairs were soon set up in the area, reaching their heyday in the 1960's. Since then the resort has declined and the town's previous glitter now looks a little tarnished.

The coast of North Wales must have been a jinx for submarines because, prior to the disaster of the 'Thetis', an earlier submarine called the 'Resurgam' was lost off the coast of Rhyl. Fortunately on this occasion there was no loss of life. The 'Resurgam' was the world's first power driven submarine, using a revolutionary design of steam engine. She was the invention of the Reverend George Garret. The vessel was built at the yards of Cochrans Iron works at Birkenhead, weighed 38 tons and was 45ft long. After launching the submarine, the plan was to tow her to Portsmouth. In the February of

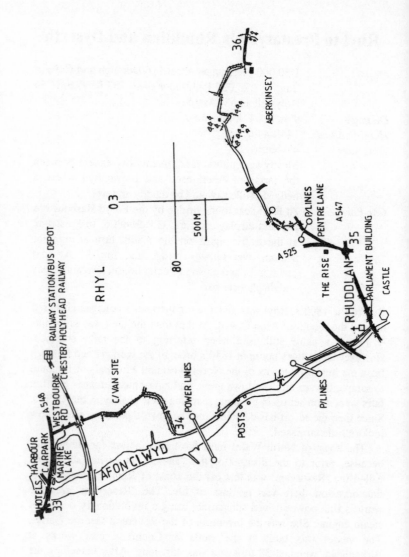

RHYL

AFON CLWYD

HOTELS
HARBOUR
CARPARK
33
MARINE
LAKE
A548
WESTBOURNE
RD
RAILWAY STATION/BUS DEPOT
CHESTER/HOLYHEAD RAILWAY
C/VAN SITE
34
POWER LINES
POSTS
P/LINES
36
ABERKINSEY
P/LINES
PENTRE LANE
A547
A525
THE RISE
RHUDDLAN
35
PARLIAMENT BUILDING
CASTLE

80   03
500M

54

1880 a flotilla set sail, but a gale sprang up and the 'Resurgam' sank whilst off the coast near Rhyl. The submarine lay in twenty metres of water, undetected, until a few years ago when a local diver was asked to retrieve tangled nets for a fishing boat. Since then the "Resurgam" has generated renewed interest and there is talk of attempts to refloat the historic vessel.

The walk now follows Afon Clwyd inland to the town of Rhuddlan, where Edward 1st built one of his many castles. If time allows, the diversion to view the castle would be worth while. Later the footpath crosses through agricultural land before it reaches Dyserth, where one can pause to view the sixty foot waterfall. This natural phenomena requires payment of a fee before it can be viewed. Dyserth also had a castle, built by Henry III in 1241 and erected on the site of an earlier fort. Like many castles in this area it fell to the Welsh Princes, when on the 4th August 1263, Llywelyn ap Gruffudd (Llywelyn II) and Gruffudd ap Madog stormed and destroyed it.

From Dyserth to Prestatyn the footpath runs along the old bed of the Prestatyn to Dyserth railway. This particular area of North Wales is rich in mineral bearing rocks, specifically the Carboniferous limestone outcrops which run from Dyserth in the north to the Llandegla Moors in the south. Indeed, after agriculture, the mining and quarrying that took place were the principal industries of the area. Lead and zinc mines have been in existence for centuries in Meliden (Talargoch Mines), whilst limestone has been quarried along the escarpment for use as building stone and lime. The transport of these materials was confined to road and water until the arrival of the Chester to Holyhead railway in 1848. However, the mines at Meliden and Dyserth were still at a disadvantage as they did not lie on the route of the new railway. With this in mind a public meeting was held on the 17th November 1860 to discuss the matter further. The meeting was chaired by Lord Mostyn, the biggest land owner in the area at that time, and it was from this first meeting that a plan to build a railway from Prestatyn to Cwm (just south of Dyserth) first emerged. The projected cost of the project was in the vicinity of £12,000 but, as in all these cases, costs escalated to £27,000. Parliamentary approval was given on the 6th July 1866 and the line was opened to goods traffic on

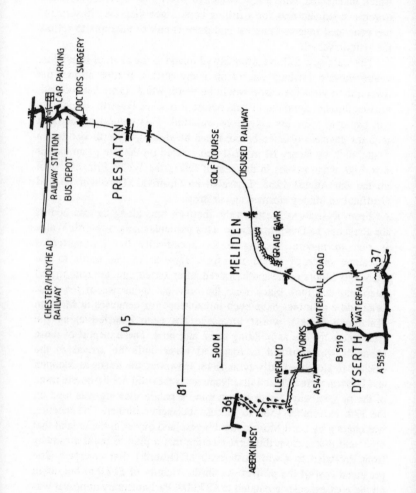

the 1st September 1869. The line was used to transport minerals, corn, coal and general merchandise, but mostly relating to the running of the mines which were at their peak in the 1870's generating considerable traffic in coal and ore. In 1896 a petition was circulated and some four thousand signatures were collected, asking for the introduction of a passenger service; but it was not until 1905 that this service became available. The inaugural run was on the 26th August 1905 with the service providing about fifteen return trips, daily. On August 16th 1930, the Prestatyn Weekly news printed the following bulletin; "The passenger service operated by the L.M.S. will be suspended at the end of the summer season, the last passenger train running on Saturday 20th September". The Red Wharf line and the Llanberis line were closed on the same day. The line now reverted to a mineral bearing track and from then there was a gradual decline of the service. The livestock facility which had been available since 1920 was withdrawn in January 1963, whilst parcel services had already gone in December 1952. Finally the line between Prestatyn and Dyserth, including the spurs to Talargoch East Works, Talargoch Main Works, Lletymwyn and Dyserth Quarry, closed completely in May of 1964. Fortunately the track bed stills remains and allows us an easy entry into the town of Prestatyn.

Walk 33. To car park entrance, and R to edge of Marine Lake. *At the time of writing major work was being undertaken around the Marine Lake and it may be necessary to walk along the road to join Westbourne Avenue where the path can be rejoined.* L along lakeside, later footpath runs L between warehouse and underground tank to road (Westbourne Avenue). R along road to end, and over railway bridge. Cross road and along road, with Auto Breakers on R, to its end. Over high wooden steps and continue on path for 12 metres, then L along caravan site boundary. Path runs between fences, passing Afon Clwyd path sign. At sign for Brickworks Pond continue along dyke with fence on R. **34.** Fence ends at river; now continue along raised section of the bank passing pipe line markers in river and, later, under new road bridge to end of embankment. Descend to lane (opposite church) and R along lane, running parallel with river to main road. L up main road

(A547), passing the Parliament House on R. Continue along to a roundabout. **35.** L along A525 keeping a watch for a large property called "The Rise" set back off the road. Here cross the road and along Pentre Lane. At a dip in the road with a small bridge, continue to gate and stile. Here, L over stile and cross field to a wooden bridge. Cross bridge and up field to top R/Hand corner. Over stile and along path running between hedges to lane. Along lane to junction and continue for a short distance to L/Hand bend, here continue down grassy track, later towards wooded area. At wood on R through gate and continue on track. At gate before cottage (Furber Court Cottage), go R with fence on L. At end of property, L over stile and continue along with hedge on L to next stile. Over this and R along field boundary to gate. Through gate and, keeping field boundary on L, cross field towards farm passing through gate to lane. **36.** L along lane to boundary of first field, and R along bridle way (can be muddy in places). Path now runs between hedges, passing through a small wooden gate. At track junction, just before bridge, L over stile and continue along field with stream on R. At field corner, close to stream, over stile and through gate onto lane. R along lane for 35 metres, then L over stile following L/Hand field boundary (stream) to sewage works. R up field to stile and main road (A547). Over stile and L along road to junction for Dyserth B5119. R across road and along Waterfall Road passing Red Lion public house on R and entrance to falls on L. Continue up Waterfall Road to junction with A5151. Here L and up hill. **37.** After hill crest, road dips and where wall on L ends, go L along path over bridge and onto railway track bed. Continue on track bed passing golf course, and following signs for Prestatyn. At track, cross roads; continue on under road bridge and into car park for doctors surgery. Cross to road and R along to main road, then L to bus station. This will bring you to the end of the North Wales Path, well done!!

Refreshments Now would seem a good time for a celebration so its off to the main shopping street in Prestatyn which provides for a variety of tastes, from Pubs to Cafes.

Accommodation B and B's in Prestatyn.

Transport At Rhyl, the bus station is situated close to the railway station in the centre of town, away from the seafront. At Prestatyn, the bus station is passed at the end of the walk, with the railway station being found slightly further on. Suprisingly for two towns so close together the service between the two can be a little bit sparse on a Sunday in winter. Bus number 36 should get you back to Rhyl or to Prestatyn (it's a circular). For timetable enquiries phone 01824 706968 or 01492 575410.

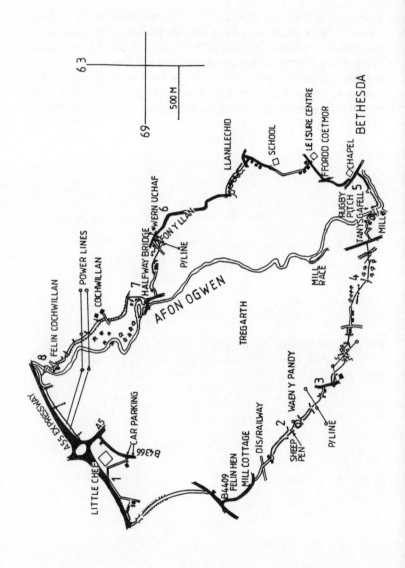

60

SELECTED WALKS

Afon Ogwen, its Mills and Tributaries

Maps:	1:50,000 Landranger sheet 115 Bangor and Caernarfon; or 1:25,000 Outdoor Leisure sheet 17, Snowdon and Conwy
Distance:	7½miles/12 kilometres.
Height gained:	440ft/134 metres.
Duration:	4½ hours.
Terrain:	Mostly good and hard, though sometimes wet in the tributary areas after heavy rain.
Car Park:	*The Little Chef* has a large car park for its customers. Two hundred and fifty metres towards Llanberis on the left hand side grass verge is an area suitable for one or two cars (G.R.593690). To reach these parking areas, from the expressway (A55) take the exit for the A5 to Bethesda and services, then on to the Llanberis Road B4366. The Little Chef is now on the R with the other two areas close by.

This excursion follows the middle reaches of Afon Ogwen and its many tributaries. The source of Afon Ogwen is at Llyn Ogwen located at the head of Dyffryn Ogwen, a mere 12 kilometres/7½miles from the sea. The river begins its journey over the spectacular water falls at Rhaeadr Benglog, and if your journey should pass this way then it is well worth the stop to view the falls, especially the drovers pack horse bridge which is not visible from the road. Park the car and find your way under Telfords road to view this little gem.

Lower down from the falls is the remains of a World War II pillbox, and this was also the site of a cattle shoeing station. Here, cattle were shod prior to their journey down to the coastal plain, and then on to the market towns on the Welsh Borders.

Afon Ogwen meanders through Nant Ffrancon (valley) before narrowing and rushing through the gorges close to the village of Bethesda. Afon Ogwen has been used by industry over the centuries, and the first account of slate being shipped from the area came in

1570, when it was recorded that slate was transported from the mouth of the Ogwen.

The walk departs from nearby the modern A55 Expressway, with its Little Chef, and explores the hinterland where many of the varied and diverse transport methods which the area has employed can be viewed. The route crosses an old L.M.S. railway line, now converted to a cycle route, whilst later, sidings for the slate railways will be passed. These were where main line trains collected slate for transport all around the country. Much of the walk follows the paths that were used by generations by the local communities on their way to, and from, their places of work. This has given the area an extensive network of paths still much in use. Sadly, although the paths remain, all that is left of the once thriving industries in the area are the romantic names on the map, such as Felin Hen (Old Mill) and Pandy (a term used for a fulling mill where cloth was thickened to make it firm and compact). Indeed, a study of the Welsh language will tell you much about the history of the area, particularly as the Welsh place names often describe the purpose and nature of the buildings.

Later the path dips down to cross under the remains of a slate railway which once ran from Penrhyn Quarry down to Bangor (Porth Penrhyn). This line carried the slate down to the quay and was used purely for quarry traffic. Later in the walk you will pass the garage for Purple Motors, a company located in Station Road. The station that was here was for passenger traffic in to Bangor. At one time the quarry was the biggest employer in the area with nearly three thousand workers. The quarry is still the biggest opencast slate workings in the world, but its work force is now much smaller.

Look out for one of the old mills as you walk along the banks of Afon Ogwen.

The walk later passes through Bethesda, a Hebrew word for *House of Mercy* which was the name given to a Non Conformist Chapel built in the area around 1820. Bethesda has had many chapels as well as a number of pubs, and both sprang up as a result of the growth of the village. This in itself was due to the development of the quarry and one can only assume that the population of the time held the chapel and the pub in equally high esteem.

After Bethesda, the walk rises to the flanks of Moel Faban, with its prehistoric settlements and burial monuments. Here can be seen views up to the Carneddau and in particular the head of Cwm Lloer, known as Ysgolion Duon. This imposing cliff was known as far back as 1639 when early botanists visited the area. Indeed, one of these early adventurers, a Mr Johnson, was taken into the area by a local guide but failed to explore its depths, because the guide claimed that the eagles which lived here were far too dangerous to allow exploration.

The walk later drops to the local land mark known as Half-Way House. This house sits beside the road bridge which crosses Afon Ogwen. The path rises up to Cochwillan Farm and Hall before again dropping to Cochwillan Mill. This is the only mill on the walk which is still in operation, producing corn. Once more over the river, and you then return to modern day living.

The Walk From your chosen parking area, walk to the minor road (G.R.593692, also one of the possible parking areas) with the No Through Road sign. Down this lane to the end. **1.** L down concreted farm lane to farm on R. Just before farm, R with all farm buildings on L; through field gate and into field now with fence on R. Down field heading towards old railway bridge (R/Hand end) to reach kissing gate. Through this and L up path, to bridge. L along bridge (now a Cycle Route) to road (B4366). Cross road and R along road to junction on L. L up road (B4409) passing Mill Cottage on L; continue for 120 metres to kissing gate on R. Through this and along metalled farm lane, passing old railway bridge on R, and continue up to farm. Pass through farm yard to field gate in top L/Hand corner of yard. Through this and along track running between wall, passing first a gate on the L and later, two gates side by side. Go through the L/Hand gate. **2.** Path now continues between walls, soon passing through sheep pen to a kissing gate. Through this and up field on grassy track, passing close to small crag on R and solitary rock post on L, to reach fence corner. Continue with fence on R to corner and stile. Over stile and immediately ½L into field. Now continue with wall on R, the footpath becoming raised, to reach a gap in a wall corner. Continue up to power line post, passing under the power lines, and on to stile. Over this and along lane to road. **3.** R up road for 75 metres to kissing gate on L. L through kissing gate and along, at first with fence on R, later running parallel to power lines. The path crosses a stream and runs through an area of gorse to a kissing gate. Through this and continue onto next kissing gate, through this and on to another kissing gate, through this and onto road. Cross road to sign 'Penyffriddoedd' on R, and continue along lane with cottages on R. Down lane and through kissing gate into field. Down field with hedge at first on L, later crossing to wall on R, and passing through another kissing gate. Continue down path to next kissing gate; go through this and enter wooded area. **4.** Shortly after the path enters the woods, take L fork and at path cross-roads, continue on down to slate wall (old quarry railway bed). Pass under this and down to road. Here R up road for 30 metres, then L down track with sign 'Tanysgafell'. At track junction, L, passing cottages on R, and at garage on L the path now runs between wall and slate fence. Through kissing gate, and path bears R around the base of a rocky outcrop to a kissing gate and bridge. Through kissing gate and L over bridge, then R, following river with works fence on L to reach a road. Continue up road with high wall on L and steel fence on R to pass coach garage (Station Road) to main road (the A5). **5.** L down road to large red chapel on R. Here, cross road and up minor road (sign indicating Leisure Centre) to road junction. Continue up Ffordd Coetmor (middle of three roads) on L/Hand side of road. Immediately after the Leisure Centre on R, go L on footpath which runs between houses and tyre depot. Later pass school on R and on to road. At sharp L/Hand bend in road, continue along walled footpath to main road. L down road for 60 metres and cross road to kissing gate on R. Through this and along with wall on R, then through kissing gate and into field. Down field with hedge on L to a kissing gate. Through this and onto road. **6.** R along road passing Wern Uchaf on R. Shortly after this, L along lane. Pass Rhiw-goch cottage on R and continue on for 40 metres, then R through kissing gate and down grassy track. Later this runs between walls to pass just to the R of a large house. At side of house, through gate and on between walls to lane. Here R down lane to L/Hand bend with a cottage just after bend. Just before cottage, R through kissing gate and down to road (the A5). Take care crossing road, and R down to bridge. **7.** Cross road and pass down path with house on L to cross a slate bridge. Follow slate fence upwards, keeping fence on L. At last slate in fence, head ½R up field to field gate. Through this and along track, with fence on R. Under power lines and through kissing gate. After two metres, L through kissing gate and down field with fence on L. Pass through several kissing gates, at first with fence on L, then later on R, to reach lane serving a water mill. Through gate and onto lane. L along lane to pass to R of garage with sign, Felin Cochwillan, and continue around to bridge. **8.** Cross the bridge, and ascend to access road. L up road to where the road swings L. Here, go R through kissing gate and cross fields with fence on R to reach stile. Over this, and follow main road around, passing road sign. With care, cross road to reach service area and return to the car park you chose.

Refreshment: There are three small tea shops in Bethesda, all up the High Street from Station Street. These are Caffi Coed y Brenin, Caffi Ogwen and the most recent, Caffi Fitzpatrick. This last one is trying hard to impress, and its pleasant and simple interior is attractive. Let's hope it survives. There are also pubs in Bethesda, of which the Douglas Arms is probably the most unusual.

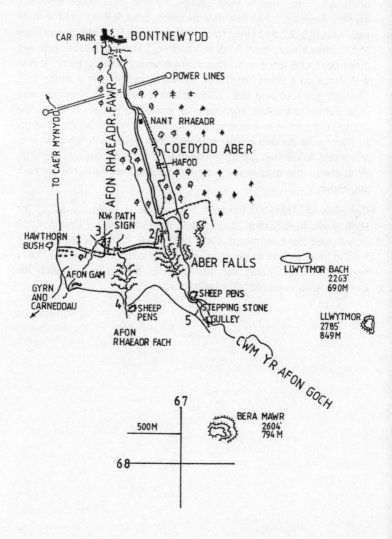

CAR PARK 🏢 BONTNEWYDD

1

○ POWER LINES

TO CAE'R MYNYDD

AFON RHAEADR FAWR

NANT RHAEADR

COEDYDD ABER

HAFOD

N.W. PATH SIGN

3

2

6

HAWTHORN BUSH ♧

ABER FALLS

AFON GAM

LLWYTMOR BACH
2263'
690M

GYRN AND CARNEDDAU

SHEEP PENS

STEPPING STONE
GULLEY

4   SHEEP PENS

5

AFON RHAEADR FACH

LLWYTMOR
2785'
849M

CWM YR AFON GOCH

67

500M

BERA MAWR
2604'
794 M

68

Aber Falls and its Drovers path

Maps: 1:50,000 Landranger sheet 115 Caernarfon and Bangor; or 1:25,000 Outdoor Leisure sheet 17 Snowdon and Conwy.

Distance: 7.5 miles/8.8 kilometres.

Height gained: 1400ft/426 metres.

Duration: 4½ hours.

Terrain: Mostly good, although wet after stile close to Rhaeadr Fach. Also wet in upper reaches of Afon Goch. **Walkers wishing to undertake this walk must be aware that a river crossing must be made of Afon Goch. This can be difficult after prolonged and heavy rain. Also, the descent close to Aber Falls is exposed in one small section.**

Car Park: Good parking at Bont Newydd G.R. 593727.

This excursion passes the spectacular Aber Falls (Rhaeadr Fawr), a haven for winter ice climbers if conditions become severe enough to allow the 120ft fall to freeze. Later, it climbs above the falls to explore its desolate source, Afon Goch.

The walk starts along a well maintained path, passing through the area known as Coedydd Aber. This is a national nature reserve, set up by the Nature Conservancy Council in 1975. The main interest in the area is for its broad leafed woodland, consisting of Oak, Alder and Ash. The Ash was, until recently, coppiced to make soles for clogs. The whole woodland is the remnant of a much greater forest which once covered the valleys and lower hillsides of North Wales. The path passes the cottage of Nant Rhaeadr which houses a detailed exhibition, and which is open from Easter to October.

Abergwyngregyn was once the home of one of the greatest of the Welsh Princes, Llywelyn ap Iorweth (Llywelyn Fawr). Llywelyn was married to Siwan (Joan), the illegitimate daughter of King John of England. During one of the many skirmishes with the English forces, Llywelyn captured an English noble named William de Braose whom he subsequently let go. Unknown to Llywelyn, however, William de

Braose and Siwan carried on an affair, and when this was discovered, Llywelyn recaptured de Braose, whom he consequently hung. Siwan died in 1237 and even though their marriage had not been without its problems, Llywelyn had her interred in great style in the Franciscan Friary at Llanfaes, near Beaumaris. When the monasteries were dissolved in 1538, her coffin was brought to the parish church in Beaumaris.

Later the walk ascends the flanks of Moel Wnion, from where there are spectacular views back towards the falls. The drovers path is now picked up, as it contours around Moel Wnion and on to Bera Mawr. This path was formed when livestock were moved from valley to valley to locate the best grazing land. There is some evidence of settlements, and also sheep pens to indicate where the livestock was gathered prior to returning to the valley floors for winter.

Above the falls, the walk enters Cwm yr Afon Goch, the source of the river over the Aber Falls. This small valley can seem very oppressed, as it is shadowed by the towering summits of Bera Mawr (794 metres) and Llwytmor (849 metres). The valley also saw wartime tragedies with the loss of two aircraft. One was a German Heinkel, with the loss of one life; the second was a Blackburn Botha, which tragically was lost with all five of its crew. The Heinkel bomber was returning from a mission to the dockyards in Barrow-in-Furness, where it was believed that the aircraft-carrier *Illustrious* was being repaired. Fortunately, she had been moved to another part of the shipyard and the ship was not damaged. The anti-aircraft fire from the guns around the shipyard had found their mark, hitting the aircraft and after the raid, the crew discovered that both the radio and compass had been damaged by shell fire. Unable to navigate accurately the plane flew into the flanks of Llwytmor, killing the engineer. The remainder of the crew survived, were captured, and sent to Prisoner-of-war camps in Canada.

Eddie Doylrush in his book *No Landing Place* gives an eerie account of a small group of aviation enthusiasts visiting the crash sites in winter. One young boy not wishing to venture into the mist, decided to investigate a nearby engine. On approaching, he noticed the figure of a man in uniform sitting on a nearby rock. The man in the uniform appeared to be carrying his head in a plastic bag and the boy screamed for his companions. As soon as one of the other enthusiasts turned up, the apparition vanished and both observers fled to the bottom of the mountain. The site they had been investigating was the final resting place of the Heinkel bomber.

August 28th 1943, saw the tragic loss of the Blackburn Botha, together with all its crew, when it flew into the side of Llwytmor in low cloud.

The path now descends, following the river through the craggy area above the falls before returning to the carpark.

The Walk 1. Out of the car park and through kissing gate (do not cross road bridge), taking lower path in woods. Up steps taking L/Hand fork, following river. Cross river over footbridge, and up to kissing gate. Through this and up to track. R along track to sharp L/Hand bend; continue on along level track (signed to Aber Falls). Continue along path passing cottage on L (Nant Rhaeadr) and pass through kissing gate. **2.** Carry on past descending path to view falls. Return to descending path and L, down to bridge. Cross bridge and up bank keeping close to fence on R. Over stile. Continue along path, later with wall on L. Cross bridge (close to Rhaeadr Fach) and cross to next stile. **3.** At North Wales Path sign, head ½L to fence; continue along fence and on to small stile. Over stile and continue along with fence on R (avoiding wet patches if possible) to fence corner. At fence corner, head straight up grassy hillside to the R of the boulders, and heading for a conspicuous hawthorn tree. At footpath, L, and follow path which descends into, and then climbs out of, a gully. Path ascends L over rocky outcrop, and later rises across the flanks of the hillside. **4.** At stream bed of Rhaeadr Fach, cross river and go up to sheep pen on opposite bank. Take small path below sheep pen, which contours around hillside and eventually reaches Cwm yr Afon Goch. Continue upstream until a deep rocky ravine is reached. **5.** Here turn around, as if to retrace your steps, and head downstream keeping close to river on R. Descend river until it divides and forms two islands. Here a crossing can be made with care. Head down stream with the path now running parallel with the river on your L. The path passes close to large sheep pens on R. Just after the pens, the river drops to the top of the falls, whilst the path contours above the river. The path descends crossing some rocky steps and gullies, where care is needed, before reaching an area of scree (loose stones). After fence on L, take the slightly rising path (difficult to spot) which crosses scree towards a gate and stile in forest edge. **6.** Path continues through forest, passing close to remains of Hafodydd, after which it emerges to rejoin the main path to the falls. R down path to field gate and kissing gate, close to road bridge; do not cross this bridge, but go L to another kissing gate. Through gate and over bridge. Path takes R/Hand fork and descends steps. Along to next kissing gate, through this, and into car park.

Refreshments A seasonal cafe can be found on L soon after entering village. The Aber Falls Hotel serves good bar meals.

Tal-y-fan from Penmaenmawr

Maps:	1:50,000 Landranger sheet 115 Bangor and Caernarfon; 1:25,000 Outdoor Leisure sheet 17 Snowdon and Conwy.
Distance:	7 miles/11.5 kilometres
Height gained:	1750ft/540metres
Duration:	5 hours
Terrain:	Mostly good firm ground, although some wet areas when crossing the open moorland. **Do not attempt this walk in mist.**
Car Park:	Parking for a limited number of cars opposite entrance to Craiglwyd Caravan Park G.R. 722759

The footpath from Craiglwyd Farm takes the steep but pleasant route up the grassy flanks of Cefn-coch, with impressive views back over the Menai Straits and Ynys Seiriol (Puffin Island). The name Ynys Seiriol is after St Seiriol, the cousin of Maelgwn Gwynedd, who set up his sanctuary on the island in the 6th century. At one time the inhabitants of the island used to catch the young puffins that also lived there, pickle them in wooden casks, and send them to England to be sold for three to four shillings a barrel. Penmon oysters were also pickled and exported. The only building on the island, besides the ruined monastery, is the remains of a Semaphore station which was in use during the last century. This was one of a number of signalling stations that extended from Holyhead to Liverpool. Ship owners in Liverpool would receive news of incoming boats by means of this chain of Semaphore stations. After falling into disuse it was converted into a biological station, but has been in ruins since the beginning of this century.

The footpath passes through the mountain wall and joins the North Wales path in an area where, during June and July, the walker is likely to see the wild Welsh Mountain Ponies descending off the higher moorland to foal, and chance encounters may surprise the walker and the mare.

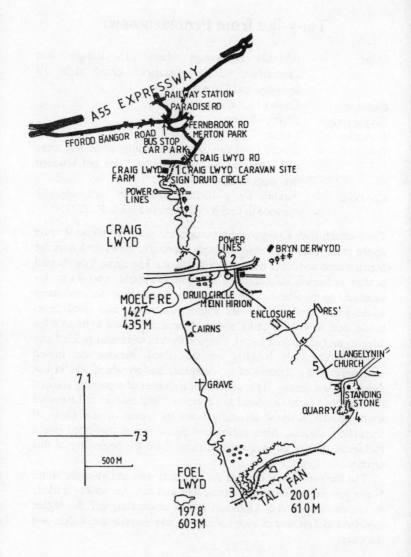

A55 EXPRESSWAY

RAILWAY STATION
PARADISE RD
FERNBROOK RD
MERTON PARK
FFORDD BANGOR ROAD
BUS STOP
CAR PARK
CRAIG LWYD RD
CRAIG LWYD 1 CRAIG LWYD CARAVAN SITE
FARM
SIGN 'DRUID CIRCLE'
POWER
LINES

CRAIG
LWYD

POWER
LINES
2
BRYN DERWYDD

MOELFRE
1427
435 M
DRUID CIRCLE
MEINI HIRION
ENCLOSURE
RES'
CAIRNS
LLANGELYNIN
CHURCH
5
71
GRAVE
STANDING
STONE
73
QUARRY
4
500 M

FOEL
LWYD
1978
603M
3
TAL Y FAN
2001
610M

As the path climbs, glance to the right towards Craiglwyd; here are the remains of a great extinct volcano, the bulk of which still dominates the town of Penmaenmawr below. This area is still being quarried for ballast for the roads and railways, but perhaps the more interesting quarrying activity here was in the Neolithic period, when the site produced stone axes. It is believed to be the third largest axe 'factory' found in the British Isles.

A short diversion can be made to view the Bronze age Druids circle at Meini Hirion. This may have been an area for recurrent rituals throughout the early Bronze age. Excavations have revealed cremation pits in which bones of children have been found. They may have been sacrificial victims to the two sinister goddesses Andros and Ceridwen, who have often been associated with this site.

The path, faint at times, winds around the open moorland to reach a saddle in the Tal-y-fan ridge line. From the moorland crest looking towards the electricity pylons, it is possible to pick out the line of the old Roman road as it heads towards Bwlch y Ddeufaen. The road ran from Caerhun (Canovium) in the Conwy valley to Caernarfon (Segontium), and was one of the best sign posted roads in Britain at that time. Relics of this and the axe factory can be seen in the museum in Bangor.

A gentle scramble brings the walker to the summit of Tal-y-fan, where magnificent views of the Conwy Valley and the Denbigh hills can be seen. Below lie the hamlets of Rowen and Caerhun. History tells us that the commander of the Roman garrison at Caerhun wed a local beauty called Elen. The garrison was the northern outpost of a Roman road constructed from Caerhun to Caerfyrddin (Carmarthen), for the movement of troops and supplies. As this ancient road is known as Sarn Helen could it possibly have been named after this local beauty? An alternative story relating to the naming of the road exists, and is mentioned in the Mabinogion. The deputy Roman emperor, Magnus Maximus was stationed in Caernarfon and was married to the beautiful Celtic princess Elen. In a dream, the Princess persuaded her husband to construct a road to link her countrymen in the south (from Caerfyrddin) with those in the north (at Caerhun). That this road exists there is no doubt and much of this paved way can still be walked, but how it gained its name is still open to speculation.

The descent from Tal-y-fan passes a now disused quarry and joins a track close to the standing stone Maen Penddu. Here, if time allows, a diversion can be made to visit the medieval church and holy well of Llangelynin. The church is open all year, with a key available if locked, from nearby Carnedd Wen. The visitors book has names from all over the world, although quite how they should find such a remote and tiny Welsh church is a mystery. The well is located in the left corner as you enter the churchyard, and is renowned for its power to cure sick children.

Walk 1. Up the road (Craiglwyd) to R. L up drive to Craiglwyd Farm (Kennels) with sign for Druid circle. Continue up, with fence on L and buildings on R. At rear of buildings a small sign for Druid circle can be found close to kissing gate. Through gate, and path climbs to L. Continue upwards with path passing a number of benches. At boggy area cross bridge/stonework, and up to a kissing gate. Through gate and R, following wall to track (the North Wales Path). L along track (here a short diversion can be made to visit the Druids Circle by going directly uphill). **2.** When track meets wall corner (building and power supply lines close by) go R and pick up track bearing R, away from wall. The path, very vague in places, climbs on to open moorland. Continue across open moorland to moorland crest. By now the path will have disappeared. Keep to the Conwy side of the ridge and here L, aiming for saddle in R/Hand flank of Tal-y-fan's ridge. Look carefully for a series of isolated cairns. Track passes the grave of Bess (a dog buried in this quiet spot). The path rises steadily in a series of curves and ,later, a small path crosses your line. Path now heads towards, and skirts, the R/Hand side of a boulder field. L across stream using stepping stones, and continue through heather to coll with wall and stile. Do not cross stile. **3.** L up to summit, keeping wall on R (to visit summit cairn, cross over at stile and recross to regain path). Continue along ridge with wall on R until the wall bears R. Here, descend ½ L (on a bearing of 35 degrees, making sure not to drop down towards Afon Conwy) and down series of small gullies to a disused quarry. **4.**

Skirt first quarry spoil heap to R, and L through quarry to join track. Descend slaty track which soon becomes a grassy track. At sweeping track junction, go L. **Here pace out 400 metres to a crucial instruction, before this the track runs downhill then sweeps right to join a broad grassy swathe** (this heads towards a small reservoir).

5. After reaching 400 metres, look for a vague track coming in from the L. At this point a vague path runs towards a notch in the skyline (three power line poles to the left of the only visible trees). Find this path and follow it towards the notch. It is easy to carry on and miss this junction, in which case you may well end up miles from your intended destination. The path is difficult to follow but keep on towards the notch. Close to the first stream is a stone circle; continue, passing this to the next stream, where a more evident path come into view. Follow this, passing close to an enclosure. This path brings the walker back to the point where the North Wales Path was left to cross the moorland at position **2.** L along track, and descend the path used for ascent.

Refreshments: The two pubs in Capelulo, the Dwygyfylchi and the Fairy Falls, with the cafe Y Bedol Bach give the nearest choices; others are to be found in Penmaenmawr (Mountain View).

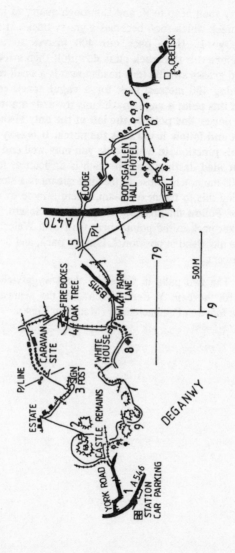

Castell Deganwy (Castle) and its Outpost

Maps: 1:50,000 Landranger sheet 115 Caernarfon and Bangor and Landranger sheet 116 Denbigh and Colwyn Bay; or 1:25,000 Outdoor Leisure sheet 17 Snowdon and Conwy.

Distance: 4 miles/6.5 kilometres

Height gained: 360ft/114metres

Duration: 4 hours

Terrain: Good and hard, perhaps a little wet in the fields and areas of long grass.

Car Park: A good car park near Deganwy railway station at G.R. 780791. As it is a pay and display car park make sure you pay for enough time. If in doubt, pay for more time.

As with many places on the North Wales coast, Deganwy owes part of its development to the Victorian era, and the coming of the train. On the initial section of the walk a covered esplanade from the Victorian period still remains. Although not quite in pristine condition, this type of covered shopping precinct is a great deal more attractive than its modern counterpart. Rising up through the residential area, you gain open countryside and the remains of Castell Deganwy, situated on two prominent outcrops, towers above you. The walk described takes you to the left of the outcrops, and allows good views of the remains of the walls in their elevated position. Further on a plaque marks the site of the gate house, whilst on the summit, the quarry that was believed to be the source of the building materials, can be seen. The remains of the castle on the summit itself are not impressive, but the importance of its strategic position will be appreciated. The views from this point take in the mighty castle at Conwy built by Edward I, leading on to Mynydd Conwy and the northern Snowdonia hills in the background. The Conwy estuary now stretches before you with its long tradition of fishing for mussels. The lives of many local families were dependent on the Conwy mussels and indeed this delicacy was famous for centuries, even being mentioned by Tacitus (the Roman historian) and poets such as Drayton and Spencer. Continuing down the estuary brings us to Llandudno and the Orme, completing the panorama from this small but significant top.

The old port at Deganwy below, was also used as a slate shipment area for the quarries in Betws-y-coed and Penmachno. However, unlike many other slate ports in North Wales, this port has been left to decay and is now in a sorry state.

It is thought that the original castle at Deganwy was constructed as a royal residence by Maelgwn Gwynedd in about A.D. 517; he even imprisoned his nephew, Elphin, in the castle. It is also believed that the first ever Eisteddfod was held in the grounds. Records show that the original structure was destroyed by lightning in A.D. 810 and destroyed by Saxons, avenging the death of their Prince Rhoderic, in 880. The castle was rebuilt by the Norman, Robert of Rhuddlan in 1080 only to be regained by the Welsh and destroyed as a result of threats by King John in his 'scorched earth policy'. The castle was rebuilt yet again by Llywelyn ap Iorwerth, but sadly on his death, his two sons were not strong enough to resist the invading English who again destroyed it in order to prevent its recapture. Henry III reconstructed the wall and towers, the ruins of which still exist today but the majority of castle was demolished by the Welsh in 1263, after a long siege by Llywelyn ap Gruffudd. As a final note to the castles' history, in 1283, Edward I whilst camping in the ruins of the castle recognised the need for a castle on the opposite bank of Afon Conwy, this idea later bringing about the construction of the great castle at Conwy. But unfortunately, due to the ferocious skirmishes that raged for over a thousand years around this site, little of the structure of Deganwy Castle now survives.

For the remainder of the walk, farmland dominates until the passage through Bodysgallen Hall estate. Here, natural woodland, including Sites of Special Scientific Interest (SSSI's), add another dimension to the walk. Bodysgallen Hall itself is now a prestigious hotel, but is once thought to have been an outpost for Deganwy Castle. Suffering a similar fate to the castle, the present building was constructed in the 17th century, although the tower itself dates back to the 13th century.

The walk continues through established woodland to where a top road gives access to an obelisk. Here, there are views up Dyffryn Conwy towards Betws-y-coed.

The Walk 1. Out of the car park and cross the main road to the covered walkway. L up road (A546) with Deganwy Castle Hotel on L. R up York Road. Follow road up hill and, where road bends R, look for wooden footpath sign on L. L up path between gardens and through kissing gate. Into field and L along path, with wall on L. After bracken ends (castle walls can be seen on R), ½ R uphill and contour around rocky outcrop to reach saddle, passing wall remains on R. Continue down to plaque. **2.** Return towards wall remains and, 10 metres before them, L up small path to summit. Return down same path to ruin. ½ R across field towards bungalows, to a stile in field corner. Do not cross stile. R with fence on L up to field gate, over stile close to field corner, and continue with fence on L. **3.** At sign post, L over stile and cross middle of field to stile and hedged lane. Over stile and along hedged lane, over stile and on with buildings on R (caravan site). Along lane to L/Hand bend, through kissing gate directly ahead and into field. R, keeping fence on R, to kissing gate in field corner. Through kissing gate and cross to caravan site road. L down road. At right hand bend, look for red fire box. Continue on to between this and the next firebox. L to stile (oak tree in hedge). **4.** Over stile and cross field with fence on L. Through kissing gate close to white house and along path between hedges to lane. L down lane (Bwlch Farm Road) to main road (B5115). Cross road and L up to crest of hill to kissing gate. R through gate and down field, with fence on L. Through next kissing gate and continue down field to gate with footpath sign. **5.** Over stile and R down road (Bodysgallen Lane) to continue to main road. Cross main road (A470) and enter drive to Bodysgallen Hall. At left hand bend, through gate and on, passing lodge on L; up lane to pass between buildings. Continue on to meet main drive, cattle grid on L. R to continue up drive, passing hotel entrance on R. Continue along wooded lane. **6.** At fork (with kissing gate on R), take L fork signed to Obelisk. Up path in woods to join road. R up road, which winds around until a footpath sign and a sign for S.S.S.I. on field gate is seen. Through this gate and up to Obelisk. Return through wood to **6.** L through kissing gate, and ½ R across field to wall. Through kissing gate and down through woods, taking left hand path to wall and fence. Over stile and down path in woods; at fork take R/Hand path, passing ornate well. Continue down with path running between walls to main road (A470). **7.** Cross road and R along footpath, through kissing gate, and into field to the R. Through next kissing gate and head gently uphill, crossing field towards a line of trees to a stile. Over stile and down field to **5.** to rejoin outgoing path to Bodysgallen Lane. L up field to main road (B5115) and L down road to Bwlch Farm Road. Cross main road and up Bwlch Farm Road. At sign for Bwlch Farm (on R gatepost) continue for 6 metres then L along path, passing between hedges. **8.** At lane (substation opposite), R up lane to sharp L hand bend. Continue on along path, over stile and uphill, with trees/fence on L to kissing gate. Through gate and continue along path which contours to R, passing under a rocky outcrop. The path goes later close to a fence corner with gates. **9.** Keep along level path, passing between two rocky outcrops, and through a metal gate. Cross field to a line of trees with gate in top corner. Over stile and L down field, with fence on left, to kissing gate. Through kissing gate and down path to road (York Road). Return to car park.

Refreshments Deganwy has two cafes, *The Vardre* and the curiously named *Hang Around*. Both are close to the car park. For those not on a budget, Bodysgallen Hall would be the ultimate. Sadly, the authors have yet to sample the quality of their refreshments!

The Bryn-y-maen Walk

Maps:	1:50,000 Landranger sheet 116 Denbigh and Colwyn Bay; or 1:25,000 Outdoor Leisure sheet 17 Snowdon and Conwy.
Distance:	4 miles/6.5 kilometres
Height gained:	540ft/155metres. The walk starts at 760ft/231 metres before descending to 216ft/66 metres, regaining height on the return trip.
Duration:	2½ hours.
Terrain:	All agricultural land, though sometimes muddy on the bottom lanes.
Car Park:	At G.R. 841752 there is room for two cars close to gateway to forestry. There is a small lay by 75 metres uphill from the church for those wishing to visit the Bryn-y-maen church.

To locate the start of the walk, leave the Colwyn Bay to Mochdre Road (A547) at a set of traffic lights with signs for the Welsh Mountain Zoo. This is the B5113 for Llanrwst, which goes up King's Drive and later Pen-y-bryn Road, before passing through Bryn-y-maen. Shortly after Bryn-y-maen, go L on the B5381 sign posted Betws-yn-Rhos. 500 metres after the turning, there is a forest on the L, park here.

This walk follows one of the last subsidiary ridge lines of the Denbigh Moors, running in a northerly direction towards the coast. The ridge offers views of the cwms of the north-eastern Carneddau, as well as the lower tops around Conwy and Deganwy, with their hill top forts overlooking the Conwy estuary. Out to sea, the coast of Ynys Môn and Ynys Seiriol provide the marine landscape.

The walk is mostly on agricultural land, following well marked footpaths along a ridge towards the outskirts of Colwyn Bay, and returning through an area of mixed woodland and then pines.

Close by the walk and well worth a visit, is the beautiful parish church of Bryn-y-maen. The church is situated in such a beautiful area that the Archbishop of Wales, during its consecration in 1899, described it as the 'cathedral in the hills'. During a visit to the church,

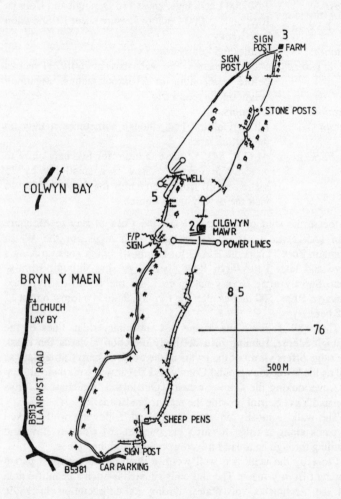

SIGN POST

3 FARM

SIGN POST

4

STONE POSTS

COLWYN BAY

WELL

5

CILGWYN MAWR

2

POWER LINES

BRYN Y MAEN

CHUCH LAY BY

F/P SIGN

8 5

76

500 M

SHEEP PENS

1

SIGN POST

CAR PARKING

B5113 LLANRWST ROAD

B5381

a short and romantic article on the history of the church, by Philip Robinson, can be purchased. It tells the story of a young girl who lived in the area who, being very poor, decided that if she ever became wealthy, she would build a church and dedicate it to the area she loved so much. The young girl was Eleanor Jones, being one of seven children who were born near the present site of the church on the Llanrwst to Colwyn Bay road. The ruins of the cottage can still be seen. Her family were very poor, and the children were sent to gather rushes from the nearby streams. These would be made into candles by the parents and sold or exchanged for goods. It was whilst visiting the local hotel to sell produce that she was noticed by two ladies who were looking for servants. An offer was made to Eleanor's mother that the ladies would take her to London to give her employment and a good education in the art of house keeping; it was an offer that Eleanor's mother found difficult to refuse. Eleanor became a credit to her benefactors, and she was introduced to the many guests who would visit the house in London. One of these visitors was the eligible bachelor Charles Frost. A romance flourished between Charles and Eleanor, and they were married in September 1863. Charles's father was James Frost, who was connected with a firm of rope and cable manufacturers. Indeed it was this company that manufactured the first communications cable that Brunels mighty steam ship, *The Great Eastern* laid from the British Isles to America. They were also responsible for the cable that the tightrope artist, Charles Blondin, used on his hair raising walk across Niagara Falls on June 30th 1859. The feat was witnessed by some 50,000 spectators.

On the death of his father, Charles inherited a considerable sum of money enabling himself and Eleanor to travel the world. Unfortunately, the only bar to their complete happiness was that they were to have no children of their own. Later life found Charles and Eleanor living in Old Colwyn and Eleanor, remembering her old, promise had a mission hall built in 1895 close to the site of the present day church. Sadly, in the year following its completion, Charles passed away. Eleanor, now with ample funds, commissioned a firm of architects, Douglas and Fordham from the Chester area, to design her a Church as a memorial to her husband. She contracted the building work to Thomas Jones of Caernarfon, and was to oversee much of the work herself. The church was consecrated on September 28th 1899 by the Archbishop of Wales. Underneath the foundation stone, placed in a sealed container, is a copy of the London Times of the date, a Jubilee Medal, and a parchment in memory of her husband. The romantic story came to a close on January 21st 1902 when Eleanor herself passed away aged 76 years. Her body was laid to rest with that of her husband. If the intention is to visit the church and it is found to be closed, a polite enquiry to the Vicarage on Colwyn Bay telephone number 01492 532567 may avoid disappointment.

The Walk At gate to forest there is a footpath sign for Colwyn Bay and a sign, *Amphlett Forest*, cross over stile and along track. After 20 metres, fork R uphill and up to stile. Over stile and into field, ½ R across field to its top corner, and cross a further two stiles. L up a grassy track. **1.** At sheep pens, R with fence on L to fence corner. L over stile and continue with fence on R. Over next stile where fence reverts to L. Path now skirts grassy bank to yet another stile. The path now runs through several fields and over several stiles, generally following the ridge line, and keeping to the path marked by yellow arrows. After another stile the path descends to a farm, passing under powerlines. **2.** Pass to the L of the farm buildings and over next stile. Head straight on and ascend a prominent hillock with a rock on top. Continue down ½ R to fence with stile, over stile, and down small valley to bottom R/Hand corner of field (trees on R). Follow fence line uphill for a short distance to field gate and kissing gate. Through kissing gate and down field, with trees on L. Path runs between two stone gate posts, before crossing large field and heading towards barns. Through kissing gate, and on with hedge on R. **3.** Close to farm buildings through kissing gate, L over stile, and along track sign posted Nant-y-glyn Road and Cilgwyn Mawr. Continue along tree lined path (do not descend from path). **4.** At field gate (sign for Ty'r Terfyn), through gate and along path lined by trees (mostly on R). At end of path, ½ L uphill with trees and bushes on L. Path rises steeply to pass under power lines; here, keep on to kissing gate (partly hidden in trees) and through this gate, with well on L. **5.** Path contours to stile in bushes, over stile, and continue along path to another stile. Over this, and immediately L through gate, then immediately R over stile (footpath sign). Descend into tree lined gully with stream in bottom. The path zigzags up hill to a stile, over this, and continue along forestry track. At Y fork in track, R down hill continuing along forestry road to track junction and gate to road.

Refreshments In Betws-yn-Rhos is the Wheatsheaf Inn doing bar snacks, restaurant meals and accommodation whilst there are many cafes in Colwyn Bay.

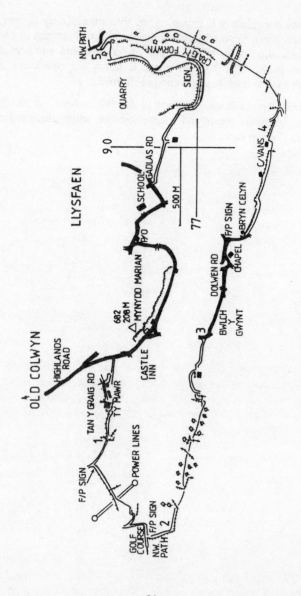

OLD COLWYN

LLYSFAEN

HIGHLANDS ROAD

TAN Y GRAIG RD

TY RAWR

CASTLE INN

682
208 M
MYNYDD MARIAN

P/O

SCHOOL

GADLAS RD

QUARRY

CRAIG FORWYN

N.W. PATH

5

SIGN

90

500 M

77

DOLWEN RD

BWLCH Y GWYNT

CHAPEL

F/P SIGN

BRYN CELYN

C/VANS

4

3

F/P SIGN

POWER LINES

GOLF COURSE

N.W. PATH

2

1

The Llysfaen Circuit (Mynydd Marian)

Maps: 1:50,000 Landranger sheet 116 Denbigh and Colwyn Bay; or Outdoor Leisure sheet 17 Snowdon and Conwy and Pathfinder sheet 736 Llandudno.

Distance: 6.5 miles/10.4 kilometres.

Height gained: The walk starts at a height of 590ft/180metres and descends to a low point of 229ft/70metres, before it climbs back to its start point.

Duration: 3½ hours.

Terrain: All agricultural land and natural woodland, although some parts can be muddy.

Car Park: Good carpark close to Castle Inn; but avoid parking close to cliffs as these are used by rock climbing groups. G.R.887775.

To locate the start of this walk, drive out of Old Colwyn on the A547. The road climbs, soon passing the Colwyn Bay Hotel (known to the locals as Hotel 70 Degrees). Shortly afterwards, take turning to R signed Llysfaen. Drive up Highlands Road for approximately ½ mile (800 metres), look for minor turning on R, Tan-y-graig Road, and follow this to the Castle Inn.

The Mynydd Marian circuit leaves the car park close to the Castle Inn. The Inn is one of the oldest public houses in the area, and is thought to date back some 300 years. Mynydd Marian is part of a limestone escarpment which stretches from Colwyn Bay in the north to Llangollen in the south. Limestone is a sedimentary rock formed about 300 million years ago. It was formed from the silt and shell remains of sea creatures settling on to the seabed. Later, huge pressures and movement pushed the rock into mountain ranges, represented today by escarpments such as this. The rock is rich in fossils, and has been much used for building stone. Indeed the quarry is thought to date back to Roman times, when it provided ballast for the many Roman roads in the area. These Roman roads were often built over, as they normally took the best route through an area. One of the Roman roads built locally now lies under the Expressway.

In the 1200's, during the reign of the last Welsh Princes, the area saw much military activity. Dafydd, the son of Llywelyn the Great, had an encampment close by, at Hwylfa Dafydd. It was from here that he held off the army of Henry III, who was on his way to Deganwy Castle in 1245. Many years later, the remains of some of Henry III's troops were found locally, sealed up in a cave. They had been entombed with their military equipment and possessions.

Later the area round Llysfaen became important for agriculture purposes. Much of the area the walk passes through belonged, at one time, to the estates of Bishop Ainan of Bangor. This powerful man was granted huge areas of land by Edward I as a reward for baptising the infant Prince of Wales. Agriculture came to dominate the area, and with it came a need to provide housing for the married farm workers. The farm workers, in most cases, had large families and were paid poor wages and consequently were forced to construct what were known as Tai Unnos. These were dwellings built during the hours of darkness, on common land, and as long as there was smoke issuing from the chimney by morning, then the farm worker was allowed to claim the land around the house. The area of land was determined by the farm worker throwing an axe from each corner of the house; the further he threw, the more land he could claim. In 1827 Lord Newborough tried to stop this practice by an Enclosure Act but to the delight of the people, he failed.

Close to the summit of Mynydd Marian was a Semaphore Station. This was part of a chain of stations stretching from Holyhead to Liverpool. The Semaphore Stations came into existence in the 1700's when Ship Owners and Merchants began to feel the need for early news of their ships and cargoes. Holyhead was a headland around which vessels bound for Liverpool had to pass, and the sailing ships could be identified whilst still at sea. The increase in sea trade, and competition amongst the ship owners, made the date and time of arrival of ships in harbour a vital piece of information. The first station was built at Bidston Hill in 1763, and a network of stations were strategically placed along the North Wales coast. By 1827 a communications network existed from Holyhead to Liverpool, a distance of some seventy miles, with twelve stations, in all, being required. The Semaphore apparatus consisted of two masts, each fitted with four arms, with two arms each side of the mast. They were operated from a room below the mast, using cones and numbers to represent the alphabet and compass directions. The operators of these stations became so expert that the Liverpool ship owners would receive information on their vessels off Holyhead in less than a minute of her number being ascertained. The speed of communication was such that the first part of the message had reached Liverpool before the last part had left Holyhead. An efficiency test was carried out in 1830 where a message was sent from Liverpool to Holyhead and the reply was received in Liverpool in the incredible time of twenty-three seconds. From 1860 the semaphore system was superseded by electrical transmissions, resulting in the closure of the intermediate stations. This was not the end of the Semaphore Station at Mynydd Marian as it was used in the early 1900's as an isolation hospital, when the area was hit by a smallpox epidemic.

The Walk Out of the car park to road, R along road to turning on L sign posted Ty-mawr. Down the drive to entrance gates. Here, down path to R of drive. On arriving at concrete path (stile in front of you), L up to farm and through farm yard to pass between two large sheds. Through gate and L to stile; over stile and R, keeping wall on R. **1.** At wall end, ½R and over stile; path now runs between hedges; when path swings to R (sign post for *Peulwys Lane*), L over stile. Follow R/Hand field boundary to pass through gate. Continue on, to pass under power lines; then ½L down very faint grassy track. The track bends R before reaching fence and drops to a T junction. L down track, passing small gates to golf course, and to gate on L with sign for the North Wales Path and Geulan Road. Over stile and down field, following grassy track. **2.** At field bottom corner, L, keeping hedge on R to next corner, with stile in trees. Over stile and cross field to wood corner, not obvious at first. Into wood at North Wales Path sign, and follow level path through woods to fence and stile. Over stile and cross field to wall stile; over stile and along path in woods, passing into next field. Cross this field to top corner with another North Wales Path sign, and into woods taking descending path to stile, close to small stream. Over this and up field to next stile and ½R to track. Here, L to gate, through this and along track which continues up to road. **3.** R along Bwlch-y-gwynt Road, at road junction up hill, now Dolwen Road, to major road junction. Up hill to pass Tabor Chapel and along Dolwen Road. At North Wales Path sign and sign for Bryn Defaid, R along track. Just after boundary wall of Bryn Celyn, L over stile and into field. Along with large wall on L and, at wall end, continue with fence on L passing cottages, and then passing close to caravan site. Over stile and pass close to stable, continuing with fence on L. **4.** Over stile and R down lane; when track bears R, go L over stile and along grassy track, until a wall corner on L becomes visible. Up to this wall corner and continue up to stile. Over stile and ½R to top of bank. Continue over crest to stile over wall. Over this and cross field, heading towards and on to ridge crest with sea behind it. Path, faint at first, heads down into woods and runs along base of scree (large crag above). **5.** At track junction (close to road), L uphill to clearing. L along path ascending to kissing gate near warning sign for quarry workings. Follow fence on R, skirting quarry, and passing through two kissing gates. At 2nd kissing gate, L along path which joins track. Continue along track to road (Gadlas Road); L to T junction, then R uphill passing school on R. At Post Office, L up Bron-y-llan Road, and at next junction continue on uphill to pass Castle Inn and return to car park.

Refreshments Seeing as the walk starts and finishes at the Castle Inn, it would be foolish not visit it.

Afon Gele and Tower Hill

Maps: 1:50,000 Landranger sheet 116 Denbigh and Colwyn Bay; or 1:25,000 Pathfinder sheet 754 Abergele.

Distance: 5 miles/8 kilometres.

Height gained: 400ft/122 metres.

Duration: 3 hours.

Terrain: Agricultural land, and in most areas good and hard, although after rain some sections may be muddy.

Car Park: Ample parking on the road side in High Street (along side the grassy play area after the turning on the L for Gele Avenue). To reach this location from the A55 Expressway, drive into Abergele to the traffic lights. Along the A547 towards Colwyn Bay for a short distance then turn L up Chapel Street/Llanfair Road A548 (signed for Llanfair Talhaiarn. and Llanrwst). There is also the George and Dragon Public house on the corner, and if travelling from Colwyn Bay this is a useful mark. Once on Chapel St/Llanfair Road, turn L opposite the Chapel on to High Street and park.

This walk starts at the small market town of Abergele which, at the moment, seems to have been taken over by the motor sales industry. The main evidence of the town being a market town for the sale of cattle and other commodities lies in the number of pubs close to the centre. One of these pubs, The Bull Hotel, has strong connections with the Mormon religion. During the renovations to the restaurant area of the hotel, the remains of a very old Mormon Chapel were discovered. This was believed to be one of the earliest Mormon Chapels in Wales, and consequently the pub has become a shrine of sorts to the followers of this religion.

The walk follows good footpaths along Afon Gele, and into the woods of Coed Abergele. Here can be seen glimpses of Abergele Hospital, once well known along the North Wales coast, and held in

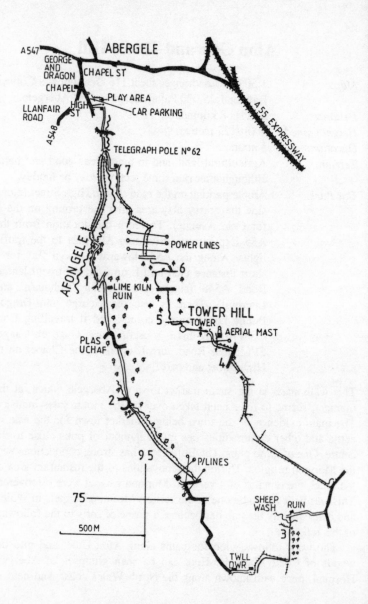

some fear. The hospital was once used as an isolation hospital for those suffering from T.B. (Tuberculosis).

Above the town is a wooded area known as Gopa Wood. The word Gopa could have been of Saxon origin meaning button, perhaps describing the shape of the hill prior to forestation. On its summit is an Iron-Age hill-fort known as Castell Cawr (Giants Castle). It consists of a single large earth bank to the south and west of the summit, with the remainder of the fort bounded against a natural cliff, the entrance being in the south-eastern corner.

The walk joins country lanes to pass Twll Dŵr which may have been the site of an old well, before descending to Afon Gele and a ruin which was a sheep wash. The ruin and the ford were used by shepherds when washing their sheep so as to 'raise' the grease from the animal's skin prior to shearing, thus facilitating the passage of the shears through the wool.

The walk ascends across agricultural lands to Tower Hill, where the old and new communication systems can be seen side by side. The new mobile phone aerial will be encountered first, whilst a little further on is the 17th century watchtower. This would have been one of a number built around the coast to warn of possible invasions from the sea.

The views from the Tower across the coastal plain, and to the estuary of Afon Gele, are quite spectacular. They also show how easily the terrible flooding in 1990 devastated the area. – see details for walk; Llysfaen to Rhyl (page 45).

The footpath now descends to rejoin Afon Gele and returns the walker to Abergele. Close to the town is Gwrych Castle, built as a folly by Lloyd Bamford Hesketh, the Duke of Dundonald – again, see details for walk: Llysfaen to Rhyl (page 45).

Close to Abergele in August 1868, one of the worst accidents to occur on this stretch of railway took place. The Irish Mail train 'The Prince of Wales' left Chester at 11.47 *en route* for Holyhead. The train was four minutes late, having taken on a further four carriages. It passed through Abergele at 12.39, trying to make up for lost time. Unknown to the driver, a goods train further up the line was manoeuvring to gain access to the sidings in Llandulas. The goods train was carrying out an illegal operation known as *fly shunting*, and this resulted in the train running away out of control down the 1:100 gradient towards Abergele. The goods train, consisting of ten wagons, two of which each contained seven and three quarter tons of paraffin loaded in fifty casks, ran down the track completely beyond control. Unfortunately, the run away train was spotted too late, and, unable to take avoiding action, the Irish Mail Train collided with the goods train while travelling at forty miles per hour. The wagons containing the paraffin rose over the locomotive and ignited on impact. The loss of life was terrible, thirty-three people perishing in the accident. Amongst them were Lord and Lady Farnham who could only be identified by the crest on their watches; some unfortunate victims were never identified.

A small white post was erected as a memorial for those who died. It was inscribed with a Cross and the date August 20th 1868. This was located on the up side of the line (Chester direction). A century later this was replaced by a two foot slate memorial with the same inscription approximately one and three quarter miles from Abergele close to the two hundred and fifteen and a half mile post. A number of victims are laid to rest in the churchyard in Abergele.

The Walk Enter field by one of two entrances (at either end) and cross to the far R/Hand corner (bungalow on R). R along metalled foot path. At road, cross over, and path now follows with stream on L. At path junction (with telegraph pole no 62), take the middle path of three. Soon the path runs with brick wall on R. Continue on, with stream on L, through kissing gate and bear L with fence to bridge. Cross bridge, and path now runs between hedges to a track junction. **1.** At track junction, L along track for 30 metres; then R up track, passing lime kiln ruin on L. At gate with sign for Plas Uchaf follow path ascending through wood. Continue on track to sharp L/Hand bend, here continue on. The path later descends through the woods to join metalled road. **2.** At metalled road, ½L crossing stream, then immediately L up path to gate and stile. Over stile and into field. Along field with boundary hedge on L, passing under powerlines and trying to avoid muddy sections, up to stile and gate. Over stile and R up lane, continue along lane ignoring junction on R. Continue along lane to sharp R/Hand bend, and here, L over cattle grid, with sign for Twll Dwr, and barns on L. Down track to bungalow and cross corner of garden, keeping fence on R, to small stile. Over this and onto next stile, then L with stream on L, and follow field boundary. Continue along field boundary to gate, through this and immediately through gate on L into field. Along edge of field following small tree lined gully on R. **3.** At end of trees, ½R down grassy bank to stream with ruin behind. R, crossing the stream and L to ruin. R along grassy track to gate; through this onto lane. L down lane and at second field gate on L, go L into field. L following field boundary to top corner of field with stile. Over this and continue on heading in the direction of the Tower on the skyline to reach next stile, in field corner. Over stile and cross field, keeping field boundary on L. Over next stile, and on with boundary on L to another stile. Over this and along with boundary fence and hedge on R and a barn on the L. Step over wire and path, now narrow, runs to road. **4.** R along road for 50 metres, then L along track running between hedges to kissing gate. Through this and R, along track passing aerial. At end of track, up field to its highest point and here cross to tower. **5.** On leaving the tower, cross over to R/Hand field boundary (seaward side). Then L, keeping fence on R, to kissing gate. Through this, and path now descends through plantation to track. L along track for 18 metres, then ½R on path down through plantation. **6.** At path junction, R, continuing down to junction on L with steps. L down steps to stile, over this and L down lane. After 40 metres, R through kissing gate. Down field keeping fence on R, and at bottom corner (ignore kissing gate), L to next field corner. Here R through kissing gate, and down footpath running between hedge and fence. **7.** At brick wall, L down to stream and R, following stream to footbridge. Over this and continue on, until path junction is reached. Here, ½R passing telegraph pole no 62, and back along the route to regain your transport.

Refreshments Situated in Chapel Street are the Kingswood House and The Farm House cafes. These appear to be the most popular cafes in Abergele. Otherwise there are a number of pubs close by.

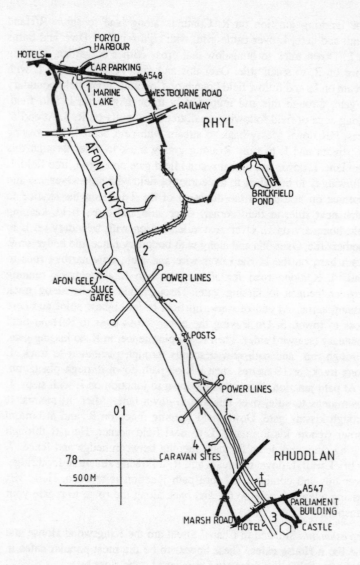

HOTELS

FORYD HARBOUR

CAR PARKING

A548

MARINE LAKE 1

WESTBOURNE ROAD

RAILWAY

RHYL

AFON CLWYD

BRICKFIELD POND

2

AFON GELE
SLUCE GATES

POWER LINES

POSTS

POWER LINES

01

78

500M

4

CARAVAN SITES

RHUDDLAN

A547

PARLIAMENT BUILDING

MARSH ROAD

HOTEL

3

CASTLE

Afon Clwyd and Rhuddlan Castle

Maps:	1:50,000 Landranger sheet 116 Denbigh and Colwyn Bay; or 1:25,000 Pathfinder sheet 737 Rhyl.
Distance:	6½ miles/10.4 kilometres, with an extra 1mile/1.6 kilometres to Brickfield Pond.
Height gained:	Negligible.
Duration:	3 hours.
Terrain:	Good and hard on dyke around estuary. At its best at high-water.
Car Park:	Rhyl, close to the harbour, in a pay and display car park G.R.996806.

The walk starts in an area known locally as Y Foryd; this was originally a cluster of fisherman's cottages, around the entrance to Afon Clwyd. In itself, this harbour had little historical importance, indeed the main port was considered to be Rhuddlan. The river was used to provide access to the castle at Rhuddlan where Edward I had a base for his Naval forces. At its peak, the force consisted of forty ships and thirteen hundred men. To enable his ships to sail up to the castle, Edward had a great dyke constructed. This was a major feat of engineering, and Afon Clwyd was canalised for three miles, the work commencing in 1277. There was even a swing bridge constructed, to enable craft to sail right up to the castle walls.

During the 17th and 18th centuries, the river was largely used to transport lead and agricultural products, whilst a large shipbuilding trade was also developing. The first recorded ship was built in 1767, being constructed for the smuggling trade. The vessel was captured off Whitehaven two years later and was later, ironically, used by Captain Gambold of Beaumaris in the fight against smugglers. 1830 saw the gradual decline of the shipbuilding industry in the river, mostly due to heavy silting. A further blow came with the construction of the Chester to Holyhead railway. A bridge was constructed over Y Foryd with a forty-five foot section which opened for the purpose of allowing vessels through to the open sea. This process took some forty minutes to complete, with ships taking precedence over trains. This situation was hardly likely to continue and in 1862 an Act was passed which allowed the railway company to permanently close the bridge. This meant that ships had to lower their masts in order to leave the river and the shipbuilding above the bridge ceased. Yards in Y Foryd basin continued to flourish until the 1900's.

The town of Rhuddlan is overshadowed by the picturesque castle standing on the banks of Afon Clwyd. The first castle in the area was built in 1015 by Llywelyn ap Seisyllt, Prince of Gwynedd, on Twt-hill. In 1156, the castle was used by Henry II as a Royal residence, but in the following year the castle was seized by Owain Gwynedd, and the English were driven out. It wasn't until 1277 when Edward I used the castle as a base against Llywelyn ap Gruffudd that the need for a new castle was realised. Edward I chose a new site and work commenced in 1277. The castle was completed as a residence for Edward and his wife Eleanor by 1281. In 1283 Edward held a Parliament in Rhuddlan in the building now known as Parliament House. This building is located on the south side of the High Street and it was here that the *Statute of Rhuddlan* was passed, one of a series of judicial changes implemented to substitute the laws of Hywel Dda with the far harder, less humane laws of Edward I and the English system.. Rhuddlan Castle came under attack twice, in 1294, and in 1400 during the uprising of Owain Glyndwr, when the castle was badly damaged but not taken.

Rhuddlan was in Royalist hands during the Civil War until it was forced to surrender to General Mytton and his troops in 1646. In order to prevent the castle from being used against them, Parliament had the castle dismantled in 1648.

As the walk passes along the embankments it is worth keeping an eye on the birdlife that inhabits this area. The estuary attracts many waders, and generally it should be possible to see Herons, Redshanks, Oystercatchers as well as Little Grebes, Shelducks and so on. The effort of carrying a pair of binoculars will generally be rewarded by the variety of birdlife seen along the dykes.

The Walk 1. At car park entrance R to edge of Marine Lake. *At the time of writing major work was being undertaken around the Marine*

Lake and it may be necessary to walk along the road to join Westbourne Avenue, where the path can be rejoined. L along lake side. Footpath runs L between warehouse and underground tank to road (Westbourne Avenue). R along road to end, and over railway footbridge. Cross road, and on along road with Autobreakers on R. At end, over wooden steps and continue on for 12 metres. Here, L along caravan site boundary. The footpath runs between fences passing Afon Clwyd sign post (ignore this). At sign for Brickworks Pond, continue along dyke, with fence on R. **2.** Fence ends at river; here, L along raised section of bank, later passing pipe line markers and under new road bridge to end of embankment. Descend to lane (opposite church) running parallel to river and follow this to main road (A547); L up main road, pausing to view the Parliament building, then R down Parliament Street, and R down Cross Street to Castle. **3.** Return from Castle to main road, L down road to bridge, and cross road to footbridge. Cross river and continue along road to pass The Marsh Warden public house. Go R after the pub along Marsh Road, passing under new road bridge and past caravan sites. **4.** At road end over stile and along track. Over stile (above sluice gates), and the path now runs on top of a grassy embankment. At embankment end, descend ½L to track, and R passing under railway bridge. Along lane to main road and at The Harbour public house, R over bridge and back to car park.

Walkers may, if they wish, make a diversion from this route to visit the reserve at Brickfields Pond. This will extend the walk by 1mile/1.6 kilometres.

Refreshments There are some cafes in Rhuddlan, plus a chip shop located in the High Street; the walk also passes The Marsh Warden, The Harbour and The Ferry public houses.

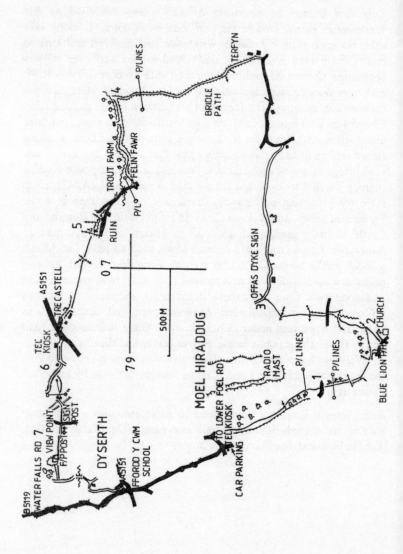

B5119 WATERFALLS RD 7

DYSERTH

VIEW POINT

F/POST SIGN POST

A5151 FFORDD Y CWM SCHOOL

TO LOWER FOEL RD

CAR PARKING

TEL/KIOSK

TEL KIOSK

A5151 TRECASTELL

MOEL HIRADDUG

RADIO MAST

P/LINES

P/LINES

BLUE LION PH

CHURCH

OFFAS DYKE SIGN

RUIN

FELIN FAWR

TROUT FARM

P/L

P/LINES

TERFYN

BRIDLE PATH

500 M

0.7

79

The Moel Hiraddug Circuit

Maps:	1:50,000 Landranger sheet 116 Denbigh and Colwyn Bay; or 1:25,000 Pathfinder sheet 755 Holywell and St Asaph.
Distance:	5½ miles/8.8 kilometres
Height gained:	360ft/109metres
Duration:	3½ hours
Terrain:	Mostly agricultural land, which can be muddy and wet along the bridle way, and from Marian Mill to Trecastell Farm.
Car Park:	At grid reference G.R.059784 in the town of Dyserth, close to a telephone kiosk, there is ample room to park on the road side. To reach this location enter on the A5151 and, at the cross-roads with the Cross Keys public house on the corner, turn along Ffordd-y-cwm. At fork, ½L up Ffordd-y-cwm, passing school on L (set back) to a minor cross-roads. Park thoughtfully near to telephone kiosk.

This walk begins in the small market town of Dyserth, which grew due to the discovery of useable rocks and minerals in the nearby Carboniferous limestone. These possessed a commercial value when processed and Dyserth, being at the northern end of an escarpment containing these rocks, soon prospered from their exploitation. This produced a boom that did not last long and quarrying now takes place on a much smaller scale than previously.

Dyserth is also well known for its waterfall. It plunges dramatically in a sixty foot fall, and can be seen by paying a small entrance fee (20p in an honesty box). It lies close to the lower road.

Situated on the southern spur of Graig Fawr, lies the site of Castell Dyserth. This was constructed in 1241 by Henry III on what was the site of an earlier hillfort. The castle was taken by storm by Llywelyn ap Gruffudd and Gruffudd ap Madog in August 1263. Sadly, nothing now remains to be seen.

The footpath also passes by an earlier defensive site. On the summit of Moel Hiraddug are the remains of an Iron-Age Hill-fort. This was some one thousand eight hundred metres long and up to one hundred and sixty metres wide. The fort had four lines of defence (separate walls protecting an inner area), and its main entrance was in the south-east. Unfortunately, due to the quarrying close to Dyserth, some of the hill fort has been lost. There are no rights of way to the summit to visit the site, but it would have had a commanding position over the surrounding landscape.

The descent into the village of Cwm passes the public house called the Blue Lion Inn. This was originally a 16th century farm house but is by now a popular pub, known for its food and a spectacular display of chamber pots which hang from the beams. In keeping with the tradition of old public houses, there is believed to be a ghost. It is reputed to be the ghost of John Henry, a farm hand thought to have been murdered in 1647. He has been blamed for several mysterious happenings in, and around, the buildings over the years.

The path climbs through a small woodland and out onto open agricultural land before joining a short section of the Offa's Dyke path. In the distance, and above the village of Trelawnyd, can be seen Gop Hill. This is surmounted by a Tumulus, known to be one of the largest of its type in North Wales. The remains of pre historic humans were found in caves around the Tumulus. One cave had the remains of a least fourteen individuals dating from the New Stone Age, and through to the Bronze age. They were found along with their implements, house hold utensils and pottery. Other bones close by belonged to both domestic and wild animals, presumably kept by the Stone Age inhabitants.

The footpath now uses bridle paths and tracks to cross over the Dyserth to Prestatyn railway track bed, before finally skirting the top of the waterfall and returning to the car park.

The Walk Walk to cross roads close to telephone kiosk and R up road, with finger post on L signed Lower Foel Road. Go up to walking man sign; here, sharp R with house "Morwylfa" on R. Along lane to end, and over home made stile. Continue along path which is now in woods. The path gradually ascends away from the houses and passes through a gap in the fence. Continue along with trees on R to pass under power lines to stile. **1.** Over stile and down to lane, cross lane and over stile into field. Cross field keeping field boundary hedge on L; under power lines to gate and stile. Over stile and down field, keeping fence on R. At fence corner continue on down field, towards wood corner. Down to gate and home made stile. Over stile and into field, now R, keeping cottage boundary on R. Go over stile and onto public road opposite pub car park. L along road passing Blue Lion Inn on R. **2.** At church gate, L over stile and into field (you have been in this one already). Follow the grave yard wall keeping it on R to top corner, here L, crossing field to stile in woods. Cross stile and into woods; the path ascends passing a well on the L, then following a stream on the R to a stile. Over this and up a small gully to a gate and road. Cross road to a crude stile on top of a wall; over stile and into field. Cross field keeping boundary fence on R to another crude stile. Over this and into next field with a concrete base close to gate. Cross field to gate; through this and cross next field to sign post. **3.** Over fence and onto grassy track (part of the Offa's Dyke Path). R along track, passing farm on R. Continue along track to reach a road. L down road to junction; here, R along road to white farm on L (Terfyn). L down bridle way to pass under power lines; here the path narrows. **4.** At valley bottom with fence corner and path junction, go L keeping field fence on L and stream on R. Path joins lane and continue on to Felin Fawr. At junction, R; here the lane joins the Offa's Dyke Path again, passing under power lines and soon passing a trout farm on R. At fork, go L and 25 metres after passing ruin on L, go R crossing stream on small footbridge, and L over stile. **5.** Cross field, keeping parallel with stream to a small bridge and stile. Over this and contour around field to gate. Through this and continue towards farm buildings ahead. Along track running between barn and hedge. Half way along this track, go R into field then L, with hedge on L to stile and main road. Cross road with care to telephone kiosk and past this to lane on R. R down lane taking L fork by gates for Long Meadow. Continue on to L/Hand bend, and here continue on over stile close to The Glen. **6.** Along lane running between hedges for 100 metres, then L, down and over stile into field. Cross stile and go ½R across field towards power lines and stile. Over stile and L onto, and over, bridge (this passes over the Dyserth-Prestatyn railway walk). At this point care must be taken to cross the field on the correct line. A ½R, crossing field to sign post, (not ½R to field corner and gate). Over metal stile and down steps to lane. Cross the lane and up concrete steps to continue along path between fences. At gate, go over stile and into field, crossing field to view point (hillock in trees). 7. From view point, L down to footpath post, then R down hill keeping trees on R to field corner. Path descends through woods to track junction. Here, L and over stile, continuing along path which later crosses concrete footbridge over stream. Ascend the concrete steps to road, then R down steps passing Glasfryn on L. At junction, continue along level path away from the concrete steps and later between walls. The path reaches the road (A5151), and here cross to the Cross Keys public house. Down road and L along Ffordd-y-cwm. At fork, go L up this road passing school (set back) on L, and finally back to the minor cross roads and telephone kiosk where the walk began.

Refreshments In Dyserth there are two public houses serving barmeals and refreshments. The Blue Lion Inn is part way around the walk, and although tempting to stop on the way, it is worth returning to this pleasant pub after the walk.

Craig Fawr and the Offa's Dyke Path

Maps:	1:50,000 Landranger sheet 116 Denbigh and Colwyn Bay; or 1:25,000 Pathfinder sheet 737 Rhyl.
Distance:	5 miles/8.0 kilometres.
Height gained:	500ft/152 metres
Duration:	3 hours.
Terrain:	Good firm walking, on the railway track bed at first; good footpath later, with dense undergrowth in some areas.
Car Park:	G.R. 064831 at the Railway Station carpark in Prestatyn. This is a pay and display carpark (at the time of writing £1 for 4 hours).

The walk starts and terminates in the attractive little town of Prestatyn. The town initially grew, during the construction of the Chester to Holyhead railway, and later became important as a tourist destination, especially for the working class families of the industrial Midlands.

The walk departs from the town following the track bed of the old Dyserth to Prestatyn railway. This railway was once important for carrying limestone products from the quarries in Dyserth, but like many branch lines was later to be closed when the line became uneconomical. Just after the beginning of the walk the path runs through the Golf links and here, a small diversion can be made to visit a Roman Bath House. To reach this turn right, passing the club house, and down to the A547 Prestatyn to Rhuddlan road. Turn right along the road, and soon left down Melyd Avenue. At the end of the avenue the remains of the Bath House may be seen. This Bath House was constructed about 120 A.D. and consisted of a hot room, into which steam was diverted in order to make the occupants sweat. Then there was a tepid room to clean the impurities from the skin, and finally a cold room, where cold baths could be taken to tone the skin. It is thought that the Bath House was constructed to cleanse those Romans who were involved in the early lead mining in the area.

Continuing the walk, the remains of Meliden (Gallt Melyd) Station will be passed and later the base of Graig Fawr, a cliff of

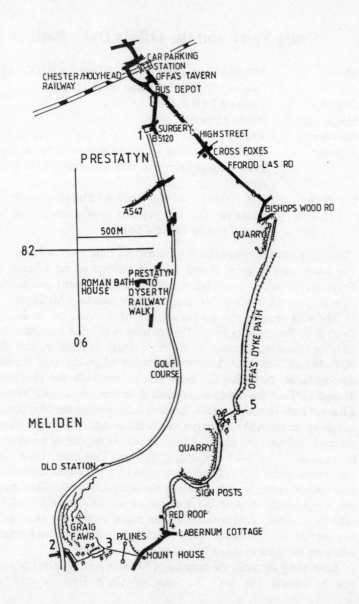

Carboniferous limestone, which is the home to many limestone loving plants. This area of unusual flora is managed by the National Trust.

The footpath now leaves the railway bed and ascends the tree lined flanks of Graig Fawr to join a grassy track to the summit. This area bears the scars of early opencast quarrying, and the bumps and ditches come from its wartime use as a tank recovery practice area. From the summit, spectacular views encompassing the Denbigh Moors, running down to the coast, and also out to sea where the Rigs supplying us with gas are clearly visible.

From Graig Fawr, the footpath returns to country lanes where the Offa's Dyke Path is joined. This is marked by the sign of an Acorn. Unfortunately the Offa's Dyke Path in this area does not run on the true Offa's Dyke, but close to what is now thought to be the Whitford Dyke. This was constructed in the 12th century and is much later than the Offa's Dyke. The Offa's Dyke was constructed by King Offa (757-796), one of the Kings of Mercia, around 784 to keep the Welsh out of England; it is in fact much further to the east, and it's true line will not be joined until the path reaches Chirk. In fact, the walk only follows the true Dyke for less than seventy miles of its entire length. Do not let this discourage you from a fine walk. Dedicated purists wishing to complete the Offa's Dyke long distance footpath in the correct manner must start, or end, the walk ankle deep in the cold waters of the Irish Sea. Likewise, at the Chepstow end of the walk, a similar ritual must be undertaken in the Severn Estuary (Aber Hafren) in order to say with confidence that the full one hundred and seventy-seven miles have been walked. Along its length the path follows natural boundaries such as rivers and cliff edges and where earth works were constructed, they can be twenty feet high and as much as sixty feet wide. This long distance path was opened in 1971 and has been enjoyed by many walkers since then; some may feel inspired by this brief wander along it to undertake the whole route. Why not?

It was noted by George Borrow in his classic *Wild Wales* that it was customary for the English to cut off the ears of every Welshman found east of the Dyke, and for the Welsh to hang every Englishman found on the western side.

Returning along the ridge, the path passes close to the village of Gwaenysgor which is famous for its parish register. This document dates back to the reign of Henry VIII, and is a remarkably well preserved register of the parish, its inhabitants and way of life.

Finally the path runs above the mixed woodland of Coedyresgob, before descending into Prestatyn to run along the High Street. Here the rucksack and boot clad walker is sure to receive some strange glances from the beach loving tourists. However, be assured that the cafes will be just as happy to accept your money as theirs.

The Walk Exit the carpark at the entrance barrier and cross footbridge over the railway. Over railway and station to pass in front of Offa's Tavern. Turn R into Bridge Road to road junction of B5120, Dyserth to Rhuddlan road. L along road, passing bus station on R. Continue to next turning on R (Doctors Surgery on corner). R down side road and L into surgery car park. Cross to far R hand corner of car park, to wooden gate and barrier. **1.** This is the termination or start of the old Prestatyn to Dyserth railway line. Through barrier and along the track. Ignore crossing paths. Later, path passes golf course and, further on again, passes the old station at Meliden (Gallt Melyd). The track bed now runs close to rocky outcrop on L. As soon as the track bed leaves this craggy outcrop, it passes over a minor road (the other side of the bridge has timber buildings close by). **2.** L down path before bridge, then ascend path running parallel with road, passing stile on R and Craig Fawr sign on L. Continue for 10 metres, then L up steps and path to kissing gate. Continue on up mini ridge running between bushes to clearing (houses on R just coming into view). At entrance to clearing, take the crossing path to the L. Ascend to the trig point on Craig Fawr (highest point). **3.** Return to where path enters bushes, then ½L, skirting around bushes; head towards gate in wall with large house in trees just behind (Mount House). Pass through gate to reach lane. L along lane to junction with Laburnum Cottage on corner. L along lane for 15 metres, then R along track (this is the Offa's Dyke Path and it is marked by acorns on signposts). **4.** Down track to a set of white gates with the sign, Red Roofs; here, ½R through kissing gate and along footpath in bushes, later with wall on R. Through kissing gate and continue along with fence on L to track junction (here with sign post). Continue on, signed for Prestatyn, and at next junction with sign post, go L. Path later has fence on L as it passes above and runs along quarry rim. **5.** At sign for Coedyresgob continue to follow path signed Prestatyn. Path ascends steeply after this. At stile, L (do not cross stile), and path contours around hillside and then starts to descend down wooden steps. The path again runs along the lip of a quarry before descending to the road. Sharp L down road, passing quarry entrance, then to road junction. Here, ½R down Bishops Wood Road, which swings L and continues as Ffordd Las. At the Cross Foxes Public House, cross the A547 road, and down Prestatyn High Street returning to car park.

Refreshments There are many cafes on the High Street in Prestatyn, as well as public houses. Eva's Pantry at the lower end is good for snacks.

The Walk from Prestatyn to Bangor

This section of the book contains all the directions you need to complete the walk from Prestatyn to Bangor. However, it does not contain the information about distance, height gain, maps etc: these are contained in the first part of the book. Please refer to these early chapters for the full information on the walk.

Prestatyn to Rhyl via Dyserth and Rhuddlan

From Prestatyn Railway Station and car parks, join the B5120 Prestatyn to Dyserth Road. Walk in the direction of Rhuddlan, soon to pass a bus station on R. Continue along to next junction on R, with Doctors Surgery on corner. Here R down road and immediately L into surgery car park. Cross car park to R hand corner and through wooden barrier onto the old Dyserth to Prestatyn Railway track. Continue along the track passing through golf course, and later past the old station at Meliden. Track now passes close to a limestone outcrop of rock. Continue on, passing under two bridges. Close to Dyserth end, the track forks L towards old station buildings; here follow path R to timber railed bridge. At end of bridge, L up to main road (the A5151). **37.** R up road and over hill crest. Road now descends through village. At edge of village, by cross roads with pub on corner (Cross Keys), R down Waterfall Road (the B5119). This later passes the entrance to the Waterfall on the R and the Red Lion public house on the L. Continue along Waterfall Road to next major road junction. Here, L along main road (A547) passing coach depot on L. Cross over road and continue, passing sewage works on R. Just after sewage works boundary fence, R over stile and down field with fence on R to stream. L keeping stream on R to fence and stile. Over this and R down lane for 35 metres to gate on L. Through this and on to stile. Over stile and along field with stream on L. At bottom corner of field, over stile and R. Path now runs between hedges and can be muddy in places. Later through wooden gate. Continue along path to lane. **36.** L along lane to sharp L/Hand bend with farm buildings; here R into field and follow R hand boundary passing one gate and onto a second gate in its top corner. Through gate and L, keeping field boundary on L to stile. Over stile and continue, keeping cottage boundary on R to next stile. Over this and R to a grassy track (which serves Fuber Court Cottage). L along grassy track to gate near wood corner. Through gate and along track to lane. Onto lane and along for short distance to L/Hand bend, here on along private drive (public footpath) passing large house (Bryn-y-wal) on R, to reach footpath running between hedges to a stile. Over stile and ½L down field to wooden bridge. Cross bridge and across next field to gate and stile. Over stile onto lane and R along lane (Pentre Lane) to reach the main road (A525). Cross road to a large property set back off the road (The Rise). L along road towards roundabout. **35.** At roundabout, R, passing through Rhuddlan, passing the Parliament House on L, and down to road bridge over Afon Clwyd. R just before bridge, and down lane running parallel with river on L. When level with church, L onto the embankment and R along it. Path runs along top of embankment passing under new road bridge and passing pipe line markers. Pass over several gates with stiles. **34.** At large fence which ends at the river, R, with fence on L along dyke. Close to caravan site and at sign for Pwll Dwr/Brickwork's Pond, L, with path now running between fences; the one on the R being the boundary for a caravan site. Pass sign for Afon Clwyd Walk and continue on with fence on R to a high ladder stile. Over this and L along road passing Auto Breakers on L to reach road junction. Cross road junction and over railway footbridge. Into Westbourne Avenue and continue along to a minor cross roads with a warehouse and underground tank on L. L, passing between these buildings to reach the "Marine Lake". *At the time of writing major work was being undertaken in this area and it may be advisable to carry on along Westbourne Avenue to the Main Road and turn L to cross the bridge over Afon Clwyd.* R along the lake side. **33.** Close to large road sign, ½R up path to car park entrance/exit.

Rhyl to Llysfaen

33. Walk to car park entrance/exit passing under large road sign and L to roundabout. Continue on to cross bridge over Afon Clwyd. At end of bridge, R, crossing main road (A548) to The Ferry. Just after The

Ferry, R along Southlands Road passing bungalows to reach dead end
(do not turn into Bryn Avenue). Pass through gap in fence and cross
open ground, passing two blue metal posts to reach a gap in the sand
dunes. Here, L along paved walkway with seawall on R. Continue on
passing derelict property, car park and toilets to reach the next caravan
site. At end of site, R, then L, to rejoin sea wall running along the top
of new sea defences. The path later drops to run along top of beach for
a short distance. The footpath then ascends stone ramp to gain a path
running between fence and wall, and parallel with railway line. The
path later descends down a concrete ramp to top of beach (area used as
a car park). Rejoin the promenade with sea wall on R, later passing car
parks, toilets and kiosks before descending to lane. Along this to pass
caravan site on L. At end of lane (Ty Crwn), the lane finishes and the
path runs along top of beach. Later path rises to run with boundary
fence for infill site on L. Path descends to next caravan site, here keep
to top of beach. On along beach to reach a stream on R. Keep on to
second bridge and here cross bridge. Go L, with stream now on L to
road. **32.** Go L along road, passing under bridges. At road junction
fork L, following river to pass picnic area. Over bridge and river, and
continue up Beach Road to junction with main road. R along road
(A547), over bridge and cross road to The Valentines public house. At
right hand end of pub, path takes passageway under buildings and then
runs between hedges to pass a white house on L (Braenar Caled). Up
drive to kissing gate on L. Through kissing gate and into field. Up
field, keeping hedge on R, and past stile with gate into a second field.
Through this, still with hedge on R, and up some concrete steps to
stile. R over stile and up field to next stile by road. **31.** R up road for 5
metres, then L along track. Shortly there is a fork in the track, take
lower track on L. Path later ascends to run along base of screes with
large crag above. Pass out of woods and gorse, and follow path uphill.
Just after screes finish cross small ridge, here on across field to a large
wall with stile. Over stile and continue over slight crest to wall corner
and fence with stile. Over stile and descend field, at first with wall on
R, until grassy track becomes visible ahead. Cross to track, then R
along track to stile. Over stile and R up lane to stile on L. Over this
and continue on with fence on R. **30.** Pass close to stables on R, over

stile and pass caravan site and cottage boundary on R. Continue with fence on R to large wall and follow this to stile. Over this and R up lane passing Bryn Celyn, and up to road junction with sign post for North Wales Path and Bryn Defaid. **29.** L along Dolwen Road, passing Capel Tabor (Tabor Chapel) on L. Cross major road junction and continue along Dolwen Road. Where this swings L take Bwlch-y-gwynt Road uphill. Bwlch-y-gwynt Road terminates close to a disused garage on L and grassy parking area on R, but continues as Geulan Road.

Llysfaen to Llandudno

At R/Hand bend (Geulan Road), L down track to bungalow. Through gate to "Pebi Gardens" and ½R to field gate and stile. Over stile and down track. Descend track to gate (do not go through), and R down field to corner. Here over stile and down to next stile. Over this passing over stream (can be smelly) to take ascending path in wood. Follow this to reach North Wales Path sign in top of field corner. Contour across field to enter woods. Through woods to emerge at wall stile. Over stile and cross field to next stile in wood edge. Over stile and follow vague level path in wood. At path junction, L to exit at wood corner with North Wales Path sign. Contour around field to gate and stile in far corner (not bottom one). **27.** Over stile and along with boundary hedge on L, later uphill to field corner and gate (sign for Geulan Road). Through gate, and L down track to reach stile on R onto golf course. Over stile and down field (golf course) with hedge on R to stile. Over stile and R down track to road. Cross road to field gate. Through this and ½L down golf course to stile in bottom corner of field (close to golf green). Over stile and down path running between houses (Green Lands) to road. R along road for 100 metres and cross over road. **26.** L down footpath to river, and path now follows river bank keeping the river on L at all times. Keep to the lower paths running close to river. At lane, along to road sign in wall on R signed Fairy Glen. Go L, crossing road and descend steps to a paved area. Here, R with the path passing under road and buildings. Follow path with river on L, passing folly on R. At road, cross to pedestrian walkway passing under bridges to reach end of promenade. **25.** Here the road bends to L, continue along promenade passing the Pier and soon passing through Llandrillo-yn-Rhos. Pass the tiny church of St Trillo and continue on, later passing a large isolated house on L called Odstone, and after that, the Golf Course. Just after end of Golf Course close to the start of the houses on R, down steps to top of beach. L along beach to reach a set of wooden steps. Up these and, at top, R along road passing bungalows to reach a cul de sac. **24.** At end, L up a set of steps then R along track which dips into a slight hollow before rising to follow fence to a flat area. L up incline to a kissing gate and through this on to plateau. L from plateau to a shallow gorse lined gully, and up R to run along the R hand edge of the quarry with boundary fence on L. At fence corner, L, initially following fence before path leaves fence and climbs through an area of gorse bushes. Path shortly rejoins fence. ½R away from fence towards a craggy ridge. In clearing in gorse, take the L hand path to L of top of Little Orme. Here follow old wall on L to kissing gate. Through this and follow fence on L, passing through bushes. Path later descends after small quarry remains, on R, to reach a kissing gate. Through kissing gate and R down road passing Craigside Inn on L. After passing bathing pool on R, join the promenade and follow this to Obelisk near the entrance to Llandudno Pier.

Llandudno to Conwy

23. At the access to the pier continue to pass the Grand Hotel on R and also pass the toll house (in use, but pedestrians don't have to pay). Continue along Marine Drive passing close to St Tudnos Church and later the access to the old lighthouse (now an interesting looking B and B). The road eventually descends to pass a disused toll house with beach close by, and the Gogarth Abbey Hotel on L. ½R to continue along promenade; here look out for the monument to Lewis Carol on the L. **22.** Continue along the promenade passing through a car park (sandy) and on to the top of the dunes, initially with fence on L (do not go along top of beach). Continue through large area of gorse, then the path runs close to golf course keeping close to white posts, and passing above an area of sea defences. Later, path descends R down to wooden sea defences. **21.** L to continue along the top of the pebbly beach to the start of the promenade. Continue along to cross the railway line and along Marine Crescent to the road junction with the A546. Go R, passing car park on R, and along the pavements towards Llandudno Junction. At L/Hand bend in road, take minor road (Glan-y-môr) carrying straight on towards bus depot. Close to this, R up steps to the road bridge. **20.** Pass under large road sign and continue along bridge passing over the Expressway. Down ramp and into gardens. Pass through these and at end of gardens, L up to bridge and cross over bridge into Conwy. At end of bridge, R descending to the Quay.

Conwy to Penmaenmawr

Go along the Quay away from the bridges to pass the smallest house in Great Britain. Pass under the arch in the castle walls onto the road, then, as the road bears L (close to Glanyrafon), turn R along tarmac footpath which runs close to the estuary. Later the path runs close to school boundary. At road, L along Morfa Drive to reach main road. Cross this and continue onto, and over, a railway footbridge. **19.** Continue along lane and at fork, R uphill past houses. At top of rise with car parking area on L, take R fork to a stile. Over this and continue up ascending path through slightly wooded area. At fork, take level path L (from here walkers wishing to gain the ridge line and visit the Prehistoric hill-fort of Castell Seion can part company and ascend R. Once on the ridge, go L and the line runs parallel to the North Wales Path, which can be regained at a later stage). Cross track junction close to an area of rocky slabs on the R. Continue to ascend the path passing close to a holly tree and quarried area on the R. Past second tree with path coming in from R. Later a path descends from the hill-fort on the R. The path now runs along the flanks of Mynydd Conwy and levels out meeting a broader path from the L. At path junction, R, slightly uphill. Continue along and cross the next path junction, soon bear R and cross to next path junction after that. **18.** Here the summit path rejoins the North Wales Path. R, bearing away from the wall and power lines, and along level track to join track from the R. Here the path sweeps to the L. At fork take R/Hand track. At crossing path, bear L slightly uphill to crest and continue on to pass under power lines and reach a stream. Cross stream by stepping stones close to footpath sign. L down track, which swings R and later L, to pass under an overhanging rock to reach a road. **17.** Cross road and up grassy bank to a field gate. Through this and continue with wall and trees on L to a track junction. Here, sharp R uphill and ascend meandering path, ignoring all tracks to the L. Later, track descends to a stile (at this point the track runs parallel to power lines). Over stile and straight on to track. **16.** Continue along track (still running parallel to power lines) and at sharp L/Hand bend, R crossing to wall. Continue with wall on R (still with powerlines). At track junction, just after large boulder (geologists call them *roche moutonées*), L along level path shortly passing through a wet area, and later through an area of bracken close to an enclosure and ruin. **15.** R, keeping enclosure wall on L to wall corner. Here, descend ½L to gully, crossing bridge over stream. Cross stile and up path, passing under powerlines. Continue to track junction. Here L, passing under more powerlines to reach a field gate in wall. Through gate and onto track. **14.** L along the track to pass Bryn Derwydd on R and line of trees on L At end of trees, R, and up to field gate. Through field gate and L along track, with wall on L to reach wall corner with building. Here continue along track which soon starts to dip. *Here those wishing to visit the Druids circle of Meini Hirion may do so by ascending ½L, crossing a small gully and on to a broad plateau. To continue the walk there is no need to retrace steps, just carry on along to regain the North Wales Path close to a wall coming up from the R.* On the R of the track, as it dips, is the ascending route from Craiglwyd Farm.

Penmaenmawr to Abergwyngregyn

For those joining the North Wales Path from Craiglwyd Farm, after passing kissing gate, R up to track. R along track which later runs close to wall. Near bottom of dip at track junction take R hand track close to wall. Rejoin track (here the path from Meini Hirion rejoins from the L), which bears ½L away from wall and later descends to field gate. Keep to the L hand track if in doubt. **13.** Through field gate and descend rough track with fence and later old wall on L. Through several gates to pass into a farm yard. Through this and along track to gate onto road (sharp bend with sign for ARC Northern Quarry). Down road to junction (close to entrance to Plas Heulog) and L down road. Continue down this road. This later descends into wooded area with sign for Nant y Coed. At sharp R hand bend, L to cross footbridge over stream. Up track to road. R along road, now dropping to reach next fork. Here L to continue along level road to reach grassy area on R with benches (somewhat neglected). At the start of this area, L through kissing gate and cross field to next stile (this is in an area of low bushes). Over this and path now ascends between old wall and fence to next stile. Over this and continue ½R steeply uphill, to join path at sharp bend. Continue up path to kissing gate. Through this and continue uphill. At track cross-roads, over, and continue uphill aiming to R of rocky knoll. Track later meets wall ascending from R. At wall with track junction, ½L away from wall to next track junction. Continue along track to pass close to wall corner on L and pylon on R. At track junction (Roman road) R. **11.** Down track which now runs parallel with powerlines, keeping to main track. Where track bends L with wall and pylon close by, follow track downhill. **10.** Track now descends to pass through field gate and into rough parking area. Through this and down road to bridge, (Bont Newydd) and parking area. Those wishing to terminate the walk here may join their transport at the car park, or continue down the road to Abergwyngregyn for public transport.

Abergwyngregyn to Bangor (Port Penrhyn)

9. Cross bridge into parking area (those walkers arriving from Abergwyngregyn village will come in from the opposite end and need to find a kissing gate). L and through kissing gate near bridge and along level path. Path crosses footbridge and continues to kissing gate. Through gate and R along track. Continue along track with sign (The Falls), later passing the cottage of Nantyrhaeadr on L. Continue along track to pass through kissing gate close to the falls. Just before falls, descend path R to cross over footbridge. Over this and up path with fence on R to stile. Over stile. **8.** Continue along footpath with wall on L crossing over a wooden bridge close to Rhaeadr Fach. On along footpath to stile and over this. The path bends to the R, passing through an area of small trees. Cross stream by stepping stones. 75 metres after this, at vague track junction, L uphill. Path later passes from R to L of old wall eventually entering a small gully with stream. Here R towards a field gate. Through this and uphill on a track passing through an area of hawthorn bushes. The track now rises across the hillside with good views back towards the falls. **7.** The track passes through two gates and under powerlines. After passing tin sheds on L, through next gate and immediately L to pass through a plantation of pines. Continue along track, passing over a number of stiles and contouring around hillside. The track eventually passes close to another plantation before it terminates at a field gate next to a minor road. Here there is a sign for Caerffynnon Cottage. Over stile and onto minor road. L along road ignoring road junction to R to reach the next track on the R. This is the track for Plas Uchaf Farm and is marked by a footpath sign just after passing under small power lines. R down track and through gate into farm yard. Through farm yard and at fork in track, take L/Hand track between walls to gate. Through this and continue down track into field, soon with wall and woods on R. Down track, and at next gate, through this. After 40 metres, L to pass through kissing gate. Through this and down field with wall on R to reach small footbridge. Over footbridge and pass through small woods to minor road. L up road, passing lane on L to Wern Bach. Continue up the road for 30 metres to a set of steps in the R hand wall. R up steps and through kissing gate. **6.** Continue along field with wall fence on R. Through wall gap just after powerlines. Continue with fence on R, and through second wall gap by ruin. At field gate for house, do not go through it but ½L up rise to pass close to telegraph pole. Continue on to a stream and metal stile. Over this and R in undergrowth to gap in old wall. Here L, with wall on R, to next stile. Through kissing gate and down field to next kissing gate and onto road. At minor road, R along it passing lane to Pant-y-gwair. The next junction on L is to Cochwillan Hall (sign at start of lane). Down this and onto Cochwillan

Further reading

The Best Pubs in North Wales	*Mike Dunn*
Pub Walks in North Wales	*Jim Knowles*
Geology and Scenery in England and Wales	*A E Trueman*
Offas Dykes Path	*John B Jones*
Llysfaen - Our village	*Joan M Davies*
Christ Church Bryn-y-maen	*Philip M Robinson*
Long Distance Trails	*Colin Elliott*
Conwy, The Town's Story	*Michael Senior*
Bless Them All	*Reg Chambers Jones*
No Landing Place	*Edward Doylerush*
Early Aviation in Wales	*Roy Sloan*
Wings of War over Gwynedd	*Roy Sloan*
Rumours and Oddities from North Wales	*Meirion Evans and Wayne Evans*
Supernatural Clwyd	*Richard Holland*
Wales - The Rough Guide	*Mike Parker and Paul Whitfield*
The hidden places of North and Mid Wales	*Mike Weil*
Cymru a'r Môr	*Gwynedd Archive Services*
Anglesey and Lleyn shipwrecks	*Ian Skidmore*
Bangor - Port of Beaumaris	*M. Ellis Williams*
"Thetis", The Admiralty regrets	*C Warren and J Benson*
Gwynedd - guide to Ancient and Historic Wales	*Frances Lynch*
Clwyd and Powys - guide to Ancient and Historic Wales	*Helen Burnham*
Roman Prestatyn	*Clwyd Powys Archaeological Trust*
The Chester and Holyhead Railway	*Peter E Baughan*
Blue Guide to Wales	*John Tomes*
Offas Dyke Path	*David Hunter and John Wright*

Useful addresses and telephone numbers

Information Centres
Colwyn Bay, 40 Station Rd Tel. 01492 530478
Conwy, Conwy Castle Visitors Centre Tel. 01492 592248
Llandudno, 1-2 Chapel St Tel. 01492 876413
Rhyl, Rhyl Children's Village, West Parade Tel. 01745 355068

Bus timetables

Flint area
Department of Highway,Transportation and Engineering
Flintshire County Council
County Hall
Mold
Flintshire
CH7 6NG
Tel. 01352 704035

Denbighshire area
Department of Highways and Transportation
Technical Services Department
County Hall
Mold
CH7 6GU
Tel. 01824 706968

Conwy Area
Public Transport Section
Highways and Transport Department
Conwy County Borough Council
Conwy Road
Colwyn Bay
LL28 5AX
Tel. 01492 575410

Gwynedd Area
Bus Gwynedd
Planning and Economic
Development Department
Gwynedd Council Offices
Caernarfon
Gwynedd
LL55 1SH
Tel. 01286 679535